THE OLYMPICS

The Olympics: The Basics is an accessible, contemporary introduction to the Olympic movement and Games. Chapters explain how the Olympics transcend sports, engaging us with a range of contemporary philosophical, social, cultural and political matters, including:

- peace development and diplomacy
- management and economics
- corruption, terror and activism
- the role of artists at the Games
- the challenge from social media
- the rise of human enhancement
- ethics and environmentalism.

This book explores the controversy and the legacy of the Olympics, drawing attention to the deeper values of Olympism, as the Olympic movement's most valuable intellectual property.

This engaging, lively and often challenging book is essential reading for newcomers to Olympic studies and offers new insights for Olympic scholars.

For more information please see the website for *The Olympics: The Basics*: http://olympicsbasics.eu

Professor Andy Miah (@andymiah) is Director of the Creative Futures Research Centre at the University of the West of Scotland.

Dr Beatriz García (@beatriz_garcia) is Head of Research at the Institute of Cultural Capital, University of Liverpool.

The Basics

THE OLYMPICS

THE BASICS

Andy Miah and Beatriz García

Routledge
Taylor & Francis Group

LONDON AND NEW YORK

First published 2012
by Routledge
2 Park Square, Milton Park, Abingdon, Oxon OX14 4RN

Simultaneously published in the USA and Canada
by Routledge
711 Third Avenue, New York, NY 10017

Routledge is an imprint of the Taylor & Francis Group, an Informa business

© 2012 Andy Miah and Beatriz García

British Library Cataloguing in Publication Data
A catalogue record for this book is available from the British Library

Library of Congress Cataloging in Publication Data
Miah, Andy, 1975-
The Olympics : the basics / by Andy Miah & Beatriz García.
p. cm. – (The basics)
Includes bibliographical references.
1. Olympics. I. García, Beatriz. II. Title.
GV721.5.M45 2012
796.48–dc23
2011032806

ISBN: 978-0-415-59587-2 (hbk)
ISBN: 978-0-415-59588-9 (pbk)
ISBN: 978-0-203-12941-8 (ebk)

Typeset in Aldus
by Taylor & Francis Books

Printed and bound in Great Britain by the MPG Books Grou

For Ethan

CONTENTS

PREFACE

When we were invited to write a 'Basics' book on the Olympics, we knew immediately that we wanted to create an accessible and focused, but overarching text, which would consider the intersecting worlds of the event known as the Olympic Games and the less well-known work of the broader Olympic movement. The Olympics is a subject about which there is an abundance of high-quality material available to access for free via Wikipedia, the International Olympic Committee website and other platforms such as the Los Angeles 1984 Foundation or the Olympic Studies Centre in Barcelona. As such, writing something that has not been said before, or which cannot be found freely online, but which covers the basics is a challenge. Indeed, we wanted to use this book as an opportunity to offer new insights into established, essential elements of the Olympic programme.

We also felt that there was a need for a book that would be useful to early career scholars and students, but also to the thousands of professionals who are charged with staging the Games and who are required to come to terms with its history, politics and values in a very short space of time. This temporary community of a few thousand individuals, who are charged with organizing an Olympic Games every two years, will rarely have a chance to study the Olympics, are unlikely ever to visit the modern Olympic headquarters in Lausanne, or the historical and symbolic centre in Olympia and, most likely, will have never been to an Olympic Games. Yet, they are expected to make sense of the Olympic values in their working lives and inspire others to do the same, so as to ensure that the Games are made meaningful to an otherwise bewildered population. This book is also for those people.

We wanted to write a book that is historically informed, but contemporary in its approach, drawing on some of the most important debates within Olympic studies of the last three decades. Thus, our primary intention for this book is to present an engaging and focused account of the Olympics, which will provoke new insights, yet also be instructive and authoritative.

Our writing is shaped by having spent a considerable part of our careers working around and at the Olympic Games as ethnographers. We have attended each Olympic Summer and Winter Games since Sydney 2000. However, more important to our understanding of this world has been a decade of participation in the work of the Olympic movement, which includes advisory board and research selection committee roles and collaborations with a range of Olympic studies centres and scholars, and ongoing conversations with Olympic decision-makers.

This book is not an exhaustive history of the Olympics, a task that many of our contemporaries have undertaken in much longer textbooks, which we reference in recognition of their contributions. Instead, our approach has been to address key elements of the Olympic programme that are essential to know, in order to grasp its complexity and importance. Moreover, our focus intends to inspire readers to reconsider what they believe the Olympics are all about. To this end, we provide examples of debates that we think will intrigue and inspire readers to learn more about the complex, fascinating and challenging world of the Olympic movement.

At present, literature on the Olympics is concentrated on three main areas of inquiry, which converge in this book in a unique way. The first is the area of sport and leisure studies, where a range of early Olympic scholarship arose in the 1980s, often through social theorists within physical education and sports departments. This approach to Olympic studies focuses primarily on the sporting and leisure dimensions of the Olympic organizations and their practices, but in recent years has also expanded and matured to include complex discussions about sport business and event management, along with tourism studies. The second body of literature to have focused on the Olympic Games comes from a historical, anthropological and philosophical tradition, focused on its ideological origins and the significance of the Olympic symbols. The third group relates to the wider social scientific study of the Olympics and is dominated by inquiries from urban studies and human geography, media and communication studies and, increasingly, sociology. This book speaks to each of these areas, as our chapter titles aim to convey.

Like the Olympics, the geographical scope of the book is global, a feature which we regard to be a distinguishing characteristic of Olympic studies. Indeed, one of the challenges of any Olympic Games is to recognize that what it brings to a nation is an opportunity to reach out to a unique and extensive global community, though often domestic politics obscure the value that may accrue from exploiting these dimensions of the experience.

The book is accompanied by a digital resource (http://olympics basics.eu) which builds on the most advanced collaborative online publishing software available today. Importantly, the resource is structured entirely around the entries that are found within our Index. As such, for readers who would like a gateway to the issues we discuss in the book, the website is a link to a collection of important historical documents which have informed our discussions. Admittedly, one of the challenges of digital resources today is longevity – even the Olympic Games websites now disappear shortly after the end of the Closing Ceremony. To address this, our resource is managed by us and we aim to ensure that it will remain within a stable environment for the foreseeable future. This database of resources may also function as a teaching guide to supplement curricula on the Olympics. Again, we stress that it it is not an exhaustive gateway to Olympic studies, but a focused resource based on the issues discussed in the book.

In closing, we are aware that the word 'sport' may be noticeable by its absence in our table of contents and this is deliberate. The book is neither an overview of the sports world, nor an inquiry into the various dimensions of sport studies. Of course, sports and athletes' experiences are dealt with extensively throughout the text, either directly or indirectly. However, this book studies the Olympics from a broader range of intellectual lenses than just sport and we consider this to be an essential approach to understanding the Olympics. Thus, our book attempts to bring new readers to Olympic studies, while transforming the understanding of those who were already involved in researching the Games or the movement.

Andy Miah and Beatriz García

Liverpool, 2011

ACKNOWLEDGEMENTS

This book would not have been possible to write without the support of many people with whom we have shared our Olympic experiences over the years. Initially, we are grateful to those who have been instrumental to our understanding of the Olympics, notably Miquel de Moragas, Simon Eassom, Gordon Mellor and Gillian Patterson, who were largely responsible for our getting involved with the Olympics as an area of scholarly inquiry.

Next, we are especially grateful to those people whom we have met in connection with the International Olympic Academy (IOA), notably Dr Kostas Giorgiadis, Dean of the Academy, and esteemed Professors, particularly Bruce Kidd, John MacAloon, Norbert Mueller and Jim Parry. In addition, the friendships we have made through the IOA with professors, students and learned professionals have furnished us with the conviction that the Olympic movement is alive and well, both as a community of critical discourse, and as a vehicle for building opportunities of intercultural education and friendship. We are also grateful to the people with whom we have shared multiple Olympic Games (or Lausanne) experiences, particularly Jean-Loup Chappelet, Richard Cashman, Alex Hesse, Kris Krug, Nao Masumoto, Holger Preuss, Robert Scales and Kristine Toohey. While our encounters are often just at the Games, they are valued constants in our lives.

Also, we owe a great deal to those institutions which have provided financial support, either in kind or in cash, to our work on the Olympics, notably the British Academy, the British Olympic Association, the Olympic Studies Centre at the Autonomous University of Barcelona, the Olympic Studies Centre at the International Olympic Committee, the Carnegie Trust for the Universities of Scotland, the Universities China Committee in London and our universities. Our special thanks go to Jan Paterson at the British Olympic Association and Nuria Puig at the IOC Olympic Studies Centre for their continuous engagement with and support to our work.

Finally, we are very grateful to Andy Humphries at Taylor & Francis for giving us this opportunity to share what we think matters about the Olympics and, as such, allowing us to bring together our research insights from the last decade.

LIST OF ABBREVIATIONS

BOCOG	Beijing Organizing Committee for the Olympic Games
EU	European Union
IBC	International Broadcast Centre
IOC	International Olympic Committee
LOCOG	London Organizing Committee for the Olympic Games
NAMC	Non-Accredited Media Centre
NOC	National Olympic committee
OCOG	Organizing Committee for the Olympic Games
ODA	Olympic Delivery Authority
OGI	Olympic Games Impact study
OGKM	Olympic Games Knowledge Management
SOCOG	Sydney Organizing Committee for the Olympic Games
UNEP	United Nations Environmental Programme
VANOC	Vancouver Organizing Committee for the Olympic Games
WADA	World Anti-Doping Agency

HISTORY AND PHILOSOPHY

We begin our exploration of the Olympics by examining its origins, which take us back some 2,500 years to ancient Greece. The inspiration for the modern Games begins here and many of the symbols and practices that are used today have their roots within this period. As such, we will consider some of the values and rituals of the ancient Olympic Games, which chart a course from 776 BC to AD 1894 and the circumstances that led to the staging of the first modern Olympic Games in 1896. An overview of their history reveals why the Olympic Games must be treated as just one part of what is described as the Olympic *movement*, the work of which extends far beyond Olympic sports competitions, medal rankings or doping issues. Indeed, the work of the movement encompasses such areas as international diplomacy, peace advocacy and developing strategies and programmes to address a range of social concerns, such as gender equality in sport. Understanding the relationship between the ancient and modern Games, provides an insight into the relationship between the Olympics and today's global society. In turn, this insight helps to explain why the Olympic Games have become the most important mega-event of all time.

Within this introductory chapter, we discuss critical elements of Olympic history. The ancient Games provide an entry point to understanding the key Olympic symbols and rituals and their reinterpretation and revival by the founder of the modern Olympic Games, Pierre de Coubertin, in the late nineteenth century. We also consider the central structures of the modern Olympics, notably the Olympic family and the International Olympic Committee (IOC) as its leading organization, to shed light on key challenges and opportunities for the Games in present times. Next, we outline the values of modern sport, notably its emphasis on attaining world records and quantification, part of a broader process with its roots in the Enlightenment's positivist desire to measure the world around us. We also consider the rise of the Paralympic Games, which shape modern sports today and keep introducing new questions and challenges to the Olympic movement from a cultural and social perspective. Finally, we acknowledge the contribution made by the core stakeholders in the Olympic Games, the athletes.

FROM ANCIENT TO MODERN GAMES

The Olympic Games were one of four 'Pan-Hellenic' Games, which took place throughout Greece in ancient times.[1] Back then, Greece did not exist as a country but rather as a series of fiercely independent and competitive city states, which were often in conflict or at war with each other. In this context, the Games were religious celebrations that unified the states and were held in honour of the Greek gods, a belief system which was shared by people in all regions. Each of the Pan-Hellenic Games honoured one particular god and, in the case of Olympia – home to the Olympic Games – this was Zeus. The date of the first Olympic Games is widely contested and, while the first recorded Games were 776 BC, Mallon (2006) indicates that the ancient Olympic Games may have existed for several centuries by this date.

The ancient Games took place in the heart of the Peloponnese, at the sanctuary of Olympia. The excavated remains of the original Olympic stadium, temples and gymnasium can be seen today, after the English traveller Richard Chandler discovered them in 1766 (Loland 1994). One century later, in 1875, a German archaeologist by the name of Ernst Curtius began excavation. By 1936, the ancient Olympic stadium – still not fully excavated – became a part of the modern Olympic programme by acting as the location for the lighting ceremony of the Olympic flame, where the torch relay begins for all three modern Olympic Games – Summer, Winter and, since 2010, the Youth Olympic Games. While the stadium currently functions as a tourism destination, at the Athens 2004 Olympic Summer Games it was also used for one of the Olympic sports competitions, the shot put. This was the first time it had been used for an Olympic sports contest since the ancient Games.

The site of the stadium is located adjacent to the International Olympic Academy, an institution that has led the implementation of Olympic education since 1961, when it was set up by the Hellenic Olympic Committee on the basis of a proposal by John Ketseas and Carl Diem. The Academy is part funded by the Olympic Solidarity programme[2] and is also the place where the heart of Pierre de Coubertin is buried, a symbol of the importance of this location in the modern Olympic movement. Indeed, such an Academy was part of Coubertin's vision, which gave priority to the role of education in athletic development.

The ancient Games were different from the modern Games in a number of significant ways. While some of these differences are clearly apparent, others are much more subtle or less well known. However, before considering their differences, one may ask whether a comparison between the two has any value at all. After all, there may be very little meaning to derive in comparing two events that took place so far apart in time. The world is a very different place today, compared with 2,500 years ago, and one may argue that the two events have nothing meaningful to do with each other. However, there remain some striking similarities, and not just in the sense that each is centred on athletic competitions. We will argue throughout the book that the social, political and cultural value of the Olympics today trades on this association with ancient times, and the belief that there are some enduring qualities associated with the Games that have to do with ancient values and traditions that matter to civilization. Indeed, these ideas are neatly articulated in the Olympic Charter (IOC 2010a), the constitutional document of the Olympic movement, which we explore later in this chapter.

There is no better place to begin a comparison between the ancient and modern Games than with the sports themselves. While today's Games involve 26 International Sports Federations, with approximately 36 disciplines and 302 events, the original ancient

Olympic Games included only 2 competitions – the sprint (*stadion*) and the long-distance race (called *dolichos*) – though each was slightly different from today's versions of the same activities. Moreover, the dimensions of each activity varied, with the sprint taking place over a slightly longer distance than today's 100m and the long-distance race taking place on a considerably shorter route than today's marathon. As the ancient Games grew, it added new disciplines, including chariot races, horse races and the pentathlon (discus, running, wrestling, javelin, jumping). In these disciplines, we begin to see the origins of modern athletics and the programme developed to include other, more familiar activities, such as an ancient form of boxing. Our knowledge of these sports derives in large part from ancient artefacts, such as decorated pottery, which show the activities taking place.

On another note, the conditions of competition varied for athletes, as those athletes of the ancient era would compete in the nude, a condition that could be interpreted as the ancient Games' attempt at ensuring a completely equal and non-enhanced playing field. Others argue that competing in the nude was a way of acknowledging that the Games were first and foremost a celebration of the achievements of the human body, while others would note that this condition was required in order to ensure women, who were banned from the Games, did not disguise themselves as competitors. Regardless, returning to the question of nudity as a form of celebrating the human body and providing an equal playing field, a common question that is asked about these ancient athletics competitions is whether the athletes used any kind of illegal performance enhancements, as it is a common concern today. While there were no rules as such preventing it, stories of figs and mushrooms that had drug-like effects have been identified as some of the possible ways in which athletes enhanced their performances in ancient Olympia. Understandably, there was no sophisticated system of anti-doping to prevent such practices at this time. However, as in the present day, a scientific knowledge of the body existed and was developed to assist in the sports performance. For instance, athletes used olive oil upon their bodies to stave off dehydration in the hot sun of Olympia, which helped not just to retain water but also to delay fatigue (Houlihan 1999).

Beyond the sports, the ancient and modern Games also have some commonalities in their portrayal of ritual and the staging of spectacle. One may have thought that a key difference between the two would be the fact that today's Games are defined by mediation, with 99.9 per cent of people around the world experiencing the Games via a television screen or, increasingly, a computer. Indeed, the reach of contemporary Olympic opening ceremonies alone is said to have been over 1.4 billion people worldwide for the Beijing 2008 Games, making it the largest media event in history. However, the ancient Games also had their own media system. For, while the latest broadcast technology may seem very far removed from ancient Olympia, Miller (2006) describes how the ancient Games began with a competition for the *keryx* and the *salpinktes*, literally, the announcer and trumpeteer, who would serve as the public address system during the Games. This is not unlike how the staging of the modern Olympic Games begins, as it involves a contest between television corporations, who bid for the right to broadcast the Games. The public address system of the ancient Games played an essential role, particularly because of the impor- tance of communal worship during the Olympic festival. Again, this is not dissimilar to the modern Games' founding vision and their contemporary communications policy, which may be understood as a form of public service. From their inception, the modern Games were committed to fulfilling a public service role and this principle has been partly retained, despite today's hyper-commercialized Games media rights framework. Scherer and Whitson (2009) note that the core principle in awarding the rights to broadcast the Games to a given media corporation is its ability to reach as many people as possible.[3]

Another area worth comparing are the kinds of rituals that surround each Games. While in ancient times, the rituals were structured around religious ceremonies, the modern Games may be said to have replaced religion with nationhood and patriotic sentiment as the key unifying ritual. Whether it is during the opening ceremony or medal-awarding ceremonies, the modern official Olympic protocol is structured around national flags and anthems in a way that is often reminiscent of military ceremonials, particularly because of their strong patriotic undertones. The similarity between both types of ritual remains in the attempt at creating an allegiance between the public and their fellow competitors beyond simple spectatorship. Both ancient and modern Games could be said to aspire to create a sense of awe at the same time as close identification with the athletes and their achievements, be it by making them embody the qualities of the ancient Greek gods (demonstrating the degree of perfection any human being can achieve) or, as is the case today, by portraying them as national icons and role models.

However, the differences between the ancient and modern Games may be more significant than their similarities. Perhaps the most important of these differences is the fact that the modern Olympics are an international affair, involving some 205 countries. Also, they emerge from an aspiration to improve the social and political conditions of the world, as opposed to the ancient Games' focus on Greek representation alone. Moreover, today's Games are accompanied by the Paralympic Games, which take place a fortnight after the Olympic Games. This relationship has defined the last fifty years of Olympic history, while no such involvement of athletes with disabilities is apparent in ancient times. Equally, a crucial difference between the two Games is that the modern Games involve sports competitions between women – and between men and women. While women were not permitted to compete at the very beginning of the modern Games, this quickly changed and today female athletes are approximately equal in number to male athletes at both Olympic and Paralympic Games. These differences show how far the modern Games have developed in a relatively short space of time, from a competition moulded by an idealized version of the ancient rituals, involving just five nations and nine sports, to a global infrastructure involving billions of dollars of investment and unifying the interests of around twenty-six International Sports Federations.

The commercial framework within which the modern Games operate has also led to some significant differences in terms of the athletes' social role. In the ancient Games, competitors tended to represent wealthy families, nobility and top-ranking military. There has been some degree of disagreement whether these athletes could be considered amateurs, given that, according to some, they competed for a prize and at times gained considerable wealth if they were victorious (Penn Museum 2011). However, they were certainly not considered professionals and were not full-time sportsmen. The modern Olympics started placing a very strong emphasis on amateurism as a defining characteristic of the deserving Olympic athlete and thus effectively giving prominence (and restricting participation) to individuals with some means for whom sport was just a pastime. Such requirements gradually came to an end in the early 1980s and this change had a major impact on the background and treatment of athletes, who quickly became highly professionalized and in tune with the mass-mediated, commercial spectacle that we see today. In present times, the celebrity status of athletes is a defining feature of the modern sports world and a considerable amount of importance is invested in cultivating these public personas beyond them being good athletes. This is not to say that there were no celebrities in ancient times. Indeed, the achievements of all Games winners were fully chronicled and used as inspiration for songs so that they were remembered by future generations.[4] However, the meaning of celebrity in the ancient world was not intimately connected to products and brands or consumer culture, as we see today.

Other differences between the ancient and modern Games concern elements of the programme that may seem essential today, but which differ considerably from ancient times. For instance, no medals were awarded to the victors at the ancient Olympic Games and it was only first place that mattered. Winners were presented with a palm tree branch and a crown made of olive leaves to symbolize their victory. Also, in ancient times there was no quantitative record-keeping of the results. As Guttmann (1978) describes, the obsession to record the results of athletic accomplishments is an entirely modern fascination. Guttmann's thesis reveals that the values of contemporary sport could be otherwise, because what mattered more in ancient times was the ritual. Indeed, the modern-day desire to record results stems from the internationalization of sports, which rely on comparisons between athletes and across nations, in order to establish a hierarchy and selection system for international competitions.

In terms of duration and location, the differences are also clear. The ancient Games always took place on the same site, while the modern version moves from one city to the next. Also, while the ancient Games lasted between one and five days, today's Olympic festival involves sixteen days of competition and represents the culmination of local, national and international sports competitions and qualification events that take place over the four years that lead to an athlete's participation in the Games as part of a national delegation. Furthermore, the ancient Olympic Games included competitions in a range of cultural practices, not just sport. Indeed, the sports competitions took place over only one day of this five-day event, with the other four days devoted to religious ceremony (Mallon 2006). While cultural competitions have also taken place in the modern Games (between 1912 and 1948), this is no longer a prominent feature of today's Olympic programme. Instead, some minor cultural competitions take place, often on an ad hoc basis, while the main Olympic cultural programme is presented in the form of a non-competitive festival that is not directly linked to (certainly not embedded within) the sports programme, as discussed in Chapter 3.

Many of these features of the modern Games derive from the initial vision of its founder, French aristocrat and educator Baron Pierre de Coubertin (1863-1937), who was the first of just eight IOC Presidents who have led the Olympic movement over the last century. Coubertin's vision remains a prominent feature of the Olympic values today and his special role in developing the modern Games requires careful explanation. One of the most important aspects of how we make sense of the ancient and modern Games today is in terms of their status as more than just sports competitions. While today the elite sports industries and infrastructure dominate the Olympic community, the sports competitions are still only one part of the Olympic Games programme. This highlights the fact that, as in the case of ancient times, today's Olympic Games should be regarded as a cultural festival, rather than just a sports event. For those interested in advancing the ideas of the wider Olympic movement, the challenge for today's Games is ensuring that the operational requirements of elite sport do not overwhelm the broader aspirations attached to the Olympic values, as covered in more depth throughout the book.

PIERRE DE COUBERTIN'S OLYMPISM

Over 2,000 years passed between the end of the ancient Olympic Games and Pierre de Coubertin's revival and creation of the modern Games which began with the establishment of the International Olympic Commitee on 23 June 1894. However, Coubertin was not the first person to attempt this kind of revival (Georgiadis 2004). Some of his inspiration came from the attempts of others, notably Robert Dover in England in the seventeeth century, Dr William Penny Brookes with his Games of Much Wenlock, and Evangelis

Zappas of Greece (MacAloon 2001). Each of these revivals has a unique place in the history of the modern Olympic Games, but it was Coubertin's creation of the IOC that brought about their internationalization and eventual adoption by countries around the world. This is not to say that the modern Olympics is the only version of the Games that is still in existence today. For example, the Much Wenlock Games continue as a community athletics meeting and have enjoyed renewed attention since London won the rights to host the Olympic Games in 2012. In fact, the London 2012 Olympic mascot is named *Wenlock* in recognition of the important role Much Wenlock played in shaping Coubertin's vision.

There is much speculation about why Coubertin's vision prevailed over these other attempts to revive the Games. However, the most compelling explanations involve three crucial dimensions. First, Coubertin's vision cohered with the internationalizing movements of the nineteenth century, which included such organizations as the Red Cross, the Scouting movement and the movement to establish Esperanto as a new international language (Hoberman 1995). It also emerged within the context of the growth of World Fairs around the same period (Dyreson 2010, Roche 2000).[5] The values of such organizations and events remain present in how the IOC conducts its business alongside a range of international non-governmental organizations. For instance, the Olympic Charter gives priority to such concepts as 'rights', 'human dignity', 'non-discrimination' and the 'universal' application of the Olympic principles. Second, Coubertin's aspirations coincided with the internationalization of sports through codified rules, a process which permitted nations to compete against each other on a global scale. Finally and perhaps most importantly, Coubertin's aspirations for the Olympics transcended sports and his philosophy of Olympism may be regarded as an ideology that struck a chord with other new philosophies at the time (Sullivan and Mechikoff 2004).

At the heart of Coubertin's *Olympism* is the belief that training both the body and mind is an essential requirement to fulfil human potential. Coubertin's ideas were inspired by various school systems, but most notably that of England's Rugby School, led by Headmaster Thomas Arnold. At Rugby, the practice of what was described as 'muscular Christianity' involved both intellectual and physical development (Hughes 1993), which Coubertin witnessed first hand on numerous visits. To this end, Coubertin's vision involved a life of Olympic education, which would foster the complete human and would in turn translate into a better world. Moreover, he hoped that the athletes of the revived Games would become 'ambassadors of peace', whose pursuit of excellence would make an important contribution to society (Coubertin, cited in Müller 2004). Thus, Coubertin's vision developed into a detailed philosophical framework, outlining what he regarded to be the ideal conditions of existence. In extensive writings on Coubertin's life, Norbert Müller explains the context within which Coubertin founded the Games, part of which concerned the fact that he moved within elite social circles that would assist him in making the Games a reality and an ideological success. Such individuals as Jules Simon, co-founder of the Interparliamentary Union and the International Peace Bureau (ibid.) were advocates for Coubertin. Müller (2004) also explains how the Dominican friar Henri Didon was a central actor in assisting Coubertin to develop his belief that the Games should promote universal values. Indeed, it is through Didon that Coubertin derived the motto of the modern Olympics, 'Citius, altius, fortius', which he noticed was 'chiselled in stone about the entrance of Didon's lycee in Paris' (Loland 1994: 30).

Coubertin's vision for the Games also arrived at a time in Europe where there was no clearly dominant ideological canon, thus propelling him towards forging a new perspective for humanity's future (Müller 2004). He believed that the pursuit of an athletic life involved more than the practice of mere sport and this distinction was intimately connected to his ideas about the good life: 'Olympism combines, as in a halo, all those principles which contribute to the improvement of mankind' (Coubertin, cited in Müller 2004). Müller argues that Coubertin 'wanted mankind in the 20th century to experience sport in the harmonious interplay of physical and intellectual skills, so that – set in an artistic, aesthetic frame – it would make an important contribution to human happiness' (ibid.) The objective was to inspire people (youth, in particular) at a time of despair caused by ongoing war and social unrest.

If one examines other major international sports events it becomes clear that the ideas characterized by the word Olympism had a unique resonance at the time, but that they also position the Olympic movement as a unique system of intellectual reform with currency to this day (Loland 1994). This is not to say that other sporting mega-events such as the World Cup are not deeply connected to broader political or social aspirations, or even that the Olympic movement has been especially successful in realizing its goals. Indeed, it is apparent that sports competitions are often catalysts of socialization and cultural integration, based on the simple premise that they involve the coming together of different communities in a common endeavour of respectful competition. However, the Olympic vision, articulated through the Olympic Charter and the work it does beyond sport, further reveals how the Olympic Games go well beyond what other sports competitions have been able to achieve in advancing philosophical principles and influencing social and cultural practices.

In short, the main difference between the Olympic Games and other sports events is that the latter do not place as high an emphasis on their ideological foundations as a wider social movement and as a 'philosophy of life', as is reflected by the Olympic Charter. Such an emphasis locates the Games closer to other non-sports-focused international movements which emerged at the turn of the twentieth century, such as the Universal Exhibitions. However, the delivery of such ambitions has been varied over the course of the modern Games. While the principles of Olympism have been prominent within the work of some IOC Presidents, such as Juan Antonio Samaranch who instituted the Olympic Museum, or even the current President, Dr Jacques Rogge, who launched the Youth Olympic Games, this commitment to the wider role of Olympism has had a mixed past and an imbalanced presence in current times.

When making sense of the Games, it is crucial to remember that Coubertin's vision was directed in particular towards the 'youth of the world'. Indeed, at the end of each Olympic Games, the IOC President calls 'upon the youth of the world to assemble four years from now ... to celebrate the Games' (Rogge 2008) indicating the direct dialogue between the Olympic movement and its key community, the athletes. The launch of the Youth Olympic Games in 2010 is an indication of this ongoing commitment to the Olympic ideals of engagement with young people via the practice of sports, cultural and educational activities, beyond the pressure to deliver a financially lucrative sporting event (Torres 2010). With this in mind, we may now consider some of the primary mechanisms through which the Olympic movement's values are conveyed, reinforced and made meaningful to today's generations. As such, the next section discusses how the underlying Olympic mission and values as conceptualized by Coubertin are advanced by the Olympic movement's emphasis on ritual and ceremony.

SYMBOLS, RITUAL AND MYTH

THE GREAT SYMBOL

When attempting to make sense of the world around us, being able to interpret relevant symbols, rituals and myths can play a crucial role. This is no different in the context of an Olympic Games. Indeed, the Olympic Games and movement are heavily imbued with such motifs and these concepts underpin their social significance as well as defining our expectations of them. The Olympic symbols have been discussed in great length by historians, particularly when attempting to make sense of present-day rituals in the context of the Games' longer history. Perhaps the most important symbol is the five interlocking rings, currently known as the Olympic logo, though it is officially referred to by the IOC as the Olympic *symbol*. This difference in terminology is indicative of the fact that the IOC regards the rings not just as a brand bringing in commercial opportunities, but the embodiment of the Olympic ideals. Of course, given that commercializing the rings is at the heart of the Olympic movement today, some may argue that this raises some questions as to how well its role as the embodiment of wider universal ideals is being protected (Barney, Wenn and Martyn 2002).

Coubertin presented the design of the rings to the IOC in 1914 and their meaning has been subject to considerable debate (Lennartz 2001). The official IOC interpretation of the rings states that they represent the five continents that participate in the Games. This is not to say that each ring is associated with a specific continent, although for some years the official IOC history did make such a claim.[6] Moreover, the six colours of the symbol – the five rings and the white background – are designed as such so as to include at least one colour from the flag of every participating Olympic nation. Yet, even these seemingly simple explanations are contested.

Certainly, Coubertin indicated that: 'These five rings represent the five parts of the world from this point on won over to Olympism' (Coubertin, cited in VanWynsberghe and Ritchie 1994: 125). But it is unclear exactly whether he meant the five continents or the five host nations participating in the first modern Games (Barney 1992). The original inspiration for the rings as a design to represent the Olympics is also unclear. We know that Coubertin was involved with the Union des Sociétés Françaises des Sport Athletiques (USFSA), the logo of which is two interlocking rings, symbolizing union (Young 1985: 326). This may be the most convincing explanation of their origin, but it is not confirmed.

Over the last century, the design of the Olympic symbol has changed slightly, particularly around the spacing of the rings, but they remain very close to the 1914 original. Today, the Olympic rings are a symbol protected by the World Intellectual Property Organization's Nairobi Treaty 1981 (World Intellectual Property Organization 1981), though for countries which have not signed this agreement its protection is governed by domestic laws whereby the National Olympic Committees (NOC) hold exclusive rights to the use of the rings and a responsibility for their protection (Elcombe and Wenn 2011; IOC 2010a).

THE THREE PILLARS OF OLYMPISM

In much of the literature on the Olympics, there is a reference to the *three pillars of Olympism*, which are supposed to symbolize the key priorities of the Olympic movement. However, there is considerable debate about what these three pillars actually refer to. Importantly, they are a phrase that has emerged from the IOC, as opposed to something Coubertin expressed explicitly. In any case, Coubertin characterized Olympism as being focused on the blend of 'sport, culture and education' and this was the IOC's point of departure when choosing to emphasize the idea of three pillars (IOC 2010a). This association with pillars has been articulated in various ways over the years by different committees in the IOC. For example, in addition to Coubertin's three chosen words, which remain articulated in the same way within the Olympic Charter, the IOC website refers to 'sport, culture and the environment' as the three pillars (IOC website). Other documentation discusses

'The IOC, International Federations and National Olympic Committees' (Chappelet 2010) or the 'Olympic Games, Olympic Movement and Olympism' (documentation from the International Olympic Academy). As such, as with a great deal of the language that operates around the Olympics, there is not always a precise explanation of the meaning. Rather, words employed by various actors within the Olympic community form part of a discourse that is used for different purposes.

CEREMONIES AND PROTOCOL

There are a series of symbolic and ritualistic acts that occur within the Olympic Games programme which are primarily articulated via the Olympic ceremonies. There are a number of different ceremonies that occur around the Games period alone – the lighting ceremony, the opening ceremony, victory ceremonies, and closing ceremony. Each of these elements has strict protocol guidelines that are consistent from one Games to the next. For example, the torch-lighting ceremony always takes place within the ancient grounds of Olympia where the flame is kindled using a parabolic mirror and rays from the sun. The opening and closing ceremonies also have precisely defined elements of protocol that are prescribed by the IOC. For example, Alkemeyer and Richartz (1993: 85) remark how 'the IOC President has a time limit of three minutes for the delivery of his personal remarks'. Primary elements of the opening ceremony that are considered symbolic of the Olympic movement include the parade of participants, speeches by Olympic authorities to open the games, the playing of the Olympic anthem and host nation's anthem, the entry and raising of the Olympic flag, the last stage of the Olympic torch relay, the lighting of the Olympic cauldron, the symbolic release of pigeons, and the taking of the Olympic oath by Olympic athletes to 'play fair', to name a few of its key elements.

Opinions vary as to whether the modern forms of ceremonies have any relationship with the ancient Games, or indeed which of them have the most significance. For instance, although the lighting of the Olympic flame takes place in ancient Olympia through the re-enactment of classic Hellenic dance movements, it is not a tradition that can be fully documented back to ancient times, but is rather an interpretation of an ancient custom that originates in the 1920s and was masterminded by German sports administrator Carl Diem (see Lennartz 1997). All the same, Coubertin's vision of the Games was mindful of the importance of ceremony as a way of instilling cultural significance into the Olympic experience and borrowed from a wide range of sources to establish a memorable Olympic pageant. Thus, since their modern inception, symbols, myth and ritual have been at the heart of the Olympic festival, heightening their ritualistic dimensions compared to other sports championships (Alkemeyer and Richartz 1993). Equally, many elements of today's Olympic programme have not been in place since their beginning. For example, the torch relay was introduced for the Berlin 1936 Games – and this original act is now often referred to as having been a mechanism for Nazi propaganda, while today the torch relay is one of the important opportunities for community engagement around the Games programme.

There are other, less well-known, symbolic acts that occur around the Games which are, nevertheless, important to its history. Perhaps one of the most notable of these is the IOC President's presence in the United Nations General Assembly, where, a few months before each Games, nations are requested to cease conflicts during the Olympic period. This tradition began only in 1994, but has become a crucial means through which the IOC conveys its relationship with the UN and an important indication of its unique role within the global political sphere. Related to this is the symbolic release of doves, which is a formal part of the opening ceremony and a way of expressing the Olympic movement's aspiration towards peace.[7]

THE GAMES OF THE OLYMPIAD

When the Olympic Games began in Athens in 1896, there was only one version – the Summer Games, although some instances of these Games did include what we now regard to be Olympic Winter Games sports. From 1924, the Winter Games edition began and thus led to the hosting of two types of Olympic Games. In 2010, a third Games variation has been introduced with the Youth Olympic Games, though this remains a minor addition so far. Of the two primary Games – Summer and Winter – the Summer is the larger of the two in terms of participating countries, number of athletes and media outreach. Each involves sixteen days of competition time and is underpinned by similar protocols. However, some differences have developed between them. For instance, standard practice in an Olympic medal competition is the awarding of medals to the competitors just after the final in the venue where they have competed. Yet, since the Winter sports tend to take place in remote mountain locations not easily accessible to large sections of the population, this tradition has been modified whereby the medals are awarded to athletes later that day in a city-based venue called the 'Medals Plaza'. This tradition began at the Nagano 1998 Winter Games and the value of this change in protocol for the Olympic movement is twofold. First, the Medals Plaza creates another ticketed venue within the Olympic programme, which is also a vehicle for an integration of cultural activity and the sports ritual (the medals ceremony is usually followed by a music concert).[8] Second, bringing the athletes outside the sports venues and within a more central city location for the ceremony may create a more rewarding experience of their receiving the medal, as the staging of this ritual occurs in a more festive and relaxed atmosphere.

Each of the Games occurs within a set period known as an *Olympiad*, which consists of 'a period of four consecutive calendar years, beginning on the first of January of the first year and ending on the thirty-first of December of the fourth year' (IOC 2010a: 20). The concept of an Olympiad is taken from the ancient Games tradition, where it referred to the period of time required for athletes to train and prepare for competition. The IOC has maintained the term Olympiad to refer to the Summer Games edition. For instance, London 2012 will be the Games of the XXX Olympiad, which begins on 1 January 2012 and ends on 31 December 2015. However, the concept of 'Games of the Olympiad' is not used for the Winter Games, which are instead referred to, as in the case of Sochi 2014, as the XXII Olympic Winter Games.

Until 1992, the Summer and Winter Games took place in the same year. However, the growth of the Games as a global media event and the expansion of the sport calendar has meant that, in order to protect the commercial interests of key funders and avoid schedule saturation, they now occur approximately two years apart. The Summer Games always occur in the first year of the Olympiad, and the Winter Games in the third year. The four-year period also plays an important role within the Games' commercial agreement cycle, as global partners (both media and corporate sponsors) sign up to multi-year contracts to associate themselves with at least one Summer and one Winter Games edition at a time. This cycle operates on the basis of what is termed the Olympic *quadrennium*, which is a period different from the Olympiad, as it starts on 1 January of the year *following* the end of the respective Summer Games. For example, the present quadrennium runs from 1 January 2009 to 31 December 2012.

THE INTERNATIONAL OLYMPIC COMMITTEE AND THE OLYMPIC FAMILY

Based in Lausanne, Switzerland, the IOC is legally constituted as an international non-governmental, not-for-profit organization and is the supreme legal guardian of the Olympic movement. It was founded in 1894 by Pierre de Coubertin and, over its lifetime, it has had just eight presidents, all of whom have been men. Today, the IOC consists of 110 members, of whom nineteen are women and its Charter stipulates that it cannot grow beyond 115 members. Each member is appointed for a term of eight years, with the possibility of renewal for an unspecified number of times. IOC members tend to have had a professional sports background, are often former Olympians and are likely to have held high-ranking positions within International Sports Federations (IFs), the non-governmental organizations recognized by the IOC as administering one or more sports at world level. The IOC membership constitution now has a set of thresholds for representation, which entails a 'maximum of seventy individual members, fifteen active athletes, fifteen representatives of IFs or other associations recognized by the IOC and fifteen representatives of the NOCs [National Olympic Committees]' (IOC 2010a). The NOCs are the organizations appointed by the IOC to 'develop, promote and protect the Olympic Movement in their respective countries' (IOC website).

The work of IOC members is unsalaried and members function rather like diplomats, though their role is not to represent their nation's interests to the IOC, but rather to 'represent and promote the interests of the IOC and of the Olympic Movement in their countries and in the organisations of the Olympic Movement in which they serve' (IOC 2010a: 31). Also, IOC members may hold positions within one or more of the IOC Commissions, which have the role of 'advising the Session, the IOC Executive Board or the President' (ibid.: 47). Presently, the IOC Commissions come under the following headings: Athletes; Audit Committee; Coordination Commissions (Summer, Winter and Youth Games); Culture and Olympic Education; Entourage Commission; Ethics; Evaluation; Executive Commission; Finance; International Relations; IOC Representatives in WADA (World Anti-Doping Agency); Judicial; Marketing; Medical; Nominations; Olympic Philately, Numismatic and Memorabilia; Olympic Programme; Olympic Solidarity; Press; Radio and Television; Sport and Environment; Sport and Law; Sport for All; TV Rights and New Media; Women and Sport. While some Commissions have had a limited life, others have been around for many decades, or are Commissions that have emerged out of others. For example, the Commission for Culture and Olympic Education emerged from the previous Cultural Commission and The IOC Commission for the International Olympic Academy and Olympic Education.

The current organizational structure of the IOC involves one President, four Vice Presidents, an Executive Board of fifteen members and individual members. Its administration is under the responsibility of the Director General who, under the authority of the President, oversees the IOC's operations supported by Directors within the areas of 'Olympic Games, International Cooperation and Development, Finance and Administration, Sports, Relations with the National Olympic Committees, Technology, Communications, Information Management, Television and Marketing Services, Legal Affairs, Medical and Scientific, Olympic Museum and Olympic Solidarity' (see IOC website).

The IOC has undergone numerous transformations over the last century, though some may argue that it has not evolved enough, reacting to crises rather than proactively seeking change. Perhaps the most important of these changes occurred in the year 2000, when the IOC established a Reform Commission, following evidence that IOC members were receiving gifts from bid cities in exchange for their vote (Mallon 2000). This process brought about the creation of an Ethics Commission and a series of modifications to the IOC governance structure, including the requirement to have active athletes on the IOC, the creation of a Selection Committee to oversee IOC membership and the establishment of the Evaluation Committee which oversees Olympic Games bids. This committee is perhaps the most widely discussed aspect of the reforms, since it is the dimension that presents new guidelines for IOC members' contact with bid cities, stipulating that 'visits by IOC members to the candidate cities are not necessary' and that it should not be necessary for bid city representatives to visit IOC members (IOC 1999: 28).

The IOC main offices sit on the banks of Lake Geneva in Lausanne, just one hour from Switzerland's capital and operate out of two primary premises – the main IOC headquarters and the Olympic Museum. From humble origins as a historical archive, the current Museum was expanded and launched at a spectacular site during Juan Antonio Samaranch's Presidency. It is a vast entity providing space for tourists to interact with the Olympic exhibitions, with conference facilities and an Olympic library, which includes a studies centre and an ever-expanding multimedia documentation centre and historical archive. The IOC members are supported by a staff which has grown from twelve in 1968, to 208 in 2001 and 407 in 2007 (Chappelet and Kubler-Mabbott 2008). For an organization that is the beneficiary of multi-billion dollar contracts, this may make it seem like a thoroughly affluent community. However, over 90 per cent of this income is channelled away from the IOC towards members of the Olympic movement (NOCs, OCOGs and IFs) and this is a significant population. For instance, there are presently 205 National Olympic Committees.

Despite the IOC's prominence in directing the interests of the Olympic Games, their work is informed by the values of a broader stakeholder community, often referred to as the Olympic family. In Chapter 6, we address the organizational structures of the Olympic family in more depth, including a discussion of the relationship between the International Federations, National Olympic Committees, Organizing Committees for the Olympic Games and worldwide commercial partners. At this point, the important issue to highlight is that this Olympic community regards itself as a social movement. Again, the foundation for this claim derives from Coubertin's vision for the Olympics, but it is a view that is also shared by many scholars today. For example, Roche (2002) argues that the Olympic

movement has been the pre-eminent international cultural movement in global society in the twentieth century and appeals to the
idea, discussed earlier, that the Olympics ought not to be understood
as just a sports competition.

THE OLYMPIC CHARTER

The work of the Olympic movement is governed by the Olympic
Charter, a constitutional document first published by Pierre de
Coubertin in 1908. The Charter defines the limits of the IOC's
work as well as the values of the organization and the responsibilities of all Olympic family members. It is the definitive guide to
the fundamental issues concerning the work of the Olympic
movement and begins with the following paragraph:

> The Olympic Charter (OC) is the codification of the Fundamental Principles
> of Olympism, Rules and Bye-Laws adopted by the International Olympic
> Committee (IOC). It governs the organisation, action and operation of
> the Olympic Movement and sets forth the conditions for the celebration
> of the Olympic Games. In essence, the Olympic Charter serves three main
> purposes: a) ... is a basic instrument of a constitutional nature, [which]
> sets forth and recalls the Fundamental Principles and essential values of
> Olympism. b) ... serves as statutes for the International Olympic Committee.
> c) ... defines the main reciprocal rights and obligations of the three
> main constituents of the Olympic Movement, namely the International
> Olympic Committee, the International Federations and the National
> Olympic Committees, as well as the Organising Committees for the Olympic
> Games, all of which are required to comply with the Olympic Charter.
>
> (IOC 2010a)

The starting point for the Charter is the 'Fundamental Principles of
Olympism', which begin by stating that:

> Olympism is a philosophy of life, exalting and combining in a balanced
> whole the qualities of body, will and mind. Blending sport with culture
> and education, Olympism seeks to create a way of life based on the joy
> of effort, the educational value of good example and respect for uni-
> versal fundamental ethical principles.
>
> (IOC 2010a: 9)

It goes on to detail other aspirations such as placing 'sport at the service of the harmonious development of man, with a view to promoting a peaceful society concerned with the preservation of human dignity' and asserts participation in sport as a 'human right'. Moreover, it describes Olympism as an appeal to such values as 'friendship, solidarity and fair play', drawing attention to the unacceptability of 'discrimination with regard to a country or a person on grounds of race, religion, politics, gender'. As noted earlier, it is these values that have distinguished the Olympics historically from other organizations which emerged at the time. The Charter has been modified a number of times since its inception, with important inclusions that have further specified the limits of the IOC's work and its obligations to the Olympic family. However, perhaps most interesting is the fact that it refers to Olympism as a philosophy which blends 'sport with culture and education', reinforcing the claim that the Olympics are not defined by sports competitions alone.

THE ELITE SPORTS INDUSTRIES

Many critics of the Olympics have highlighted the ambiguity of the Olympic values, as a cause for concern. For example, the motto 'citius, altius, fortius' (faster, higher, stronger) is often misinterpreted as an explicit reference to the excess that elite athletes pursue in their attempts to do better than their predecessors or their previous performance. As we noted earlier, this motto was taken from the facade of an educational institution and historians suggest that, in fact, it appeals to far broader principles of life than the pursuit of athletic endeavour. Yet, the scientization of sport has brought about a pursuit of records, which is epitomized by a superficial reading of the Olympic motto. As such, while the modern Olympic Games now has a singular administrative infrastructure in the form of the IOC and the community over which it presides, it occurs within a larger sporting calendar which is driven by the pursuit of physical excess and the growth of the sports industries, which comprise International Sports Federations and countless sponsors who invest into the extraordinary achievements of elite athletes.

The rise of the sports federations occurred within a period of industrialization, which brought with it the development of mass participation sports experiences. Over the course of the twentieth century, sports practice shifted from an elite pursuit for the aristocracy – the period around the birth of the modern Olympic Games – to a leisure pursuit where, today, sports technologies in the high street far exceed those used by Olympians even just twenty years ago. This change in manufacturing design, the rise of the leisure class, and the gradual professionalization of elite sports participation, have also had the effect of democratizing sports culture, transforming it into a consumer product. Moreover, the growth of sport science, fracturing into specialisms in sports engineering, psychology and so on, has been underpinned by the pursuit of optimizing human performance. Hoberman (1992) provides a definitive history of this period, drawing attention to the greater prominence of sport scientists within the sports industry. In this context, twenty-first-century Olympism involves the celebration of technological excess within society, which has also defined the value of Olympic competition for the sports fan cultures and shaped how we make sense of the achievements of great Olympians.

THE OTHER GAMES

While our focus in this book is the Olympics, it would be inadequate to conclude a chapter on their history and philosophy without some reference to the Paralympic Games and other Games that have an affiliation to the modern Olympic Games. While the Paralympic Games is the most significant of these 'other Games', there are various others that take place today. For example, the Wenlock Olympian Games – one of Coubertin's inspirations – continue to take place in England, as a community sports event. Also, the International Transplant Games for athletes who have undergone some form of transplantation surgery is also a recognized affiliate of the IOC. There are also the Nemean Games, another of the ancient Pan-Hellenic Games, this time revived by Professor Stephen Miller, which recreate many of the ancient traditions, such as running barefoot. Yet, the Paralympic Games are the only other Games that operates in parallel to the Olympic Games. Their origins can be traced to Stoke Mandeville, an English town which was the site of the first games for people with disabilities. They first took place in 1948 – to coincide with the London Olympic Games that year – and were named the 'International Wheelchair Games', dedicated to world war veterans in particular. The initiative was masterminded by Dr Ludwig Guttmann, based at Stoke Mandeville Hospital, and steadily became a global, elite sports community, enjoying many of the privileges and visibility of the Olympic Games today. Often mistakenly referred to as the Para-Olympic Games, the Paraplegic Games or the Special Olympics, the Paralympic Games take place on the same biennial principle as the Olympic Games, occurring approximately two weeks after the close of the Olympic Games. Since the Seoul 1988 Summer Games and Albertville 1992 Winter Games, they are staged within the same city, using the same facilities as the Olympic Games.

There are various ways in which the Olympic and Paralympic Games are intimately connected. Perhaps most importantly, they are joined symbolically via the same Organizing Committee for the Games. However, there are also formal agreements between the IOC and the International Paralympic Committee in pursuit of a common framework of mutual support. In recent Olympic Games iterations, the programme has included Paralympic sports as show-case activities. At the Vancouver 2010 Games, part of the Olympic and Paralympic Games were concurrent, a reflection of the common policy for their support within the Canadian sports system. Furthermore, Paralympians have competed in the Olympic Games on numerous occasions. In fact, although for obvious reasons Olympic athletes are not allowed to compete at the Paralympic Games, there is nothing to stop athletes with disabilities from competing in the Olympic Games, providing they can make the qualifying threshold.

GREAT OLYMPIANS

While a comprehensive history of great Olympians is untenable for a book of this size, it is fitting to conclude this overview of Olympic history by focusing on a selection of key athletic achieve-ments which have defined the modern Olympic Games. Today, what it means to be a great Olympian is often defined in terms of quantifiable achievements and medal counts, a view which sadly neglects the other ways in which athletes contribute to society. Athletes who occupy such territory include the present Olympic swimming champion Michael Phelps, the greatest Olympian of all time in terms of gold medal wins.

Yet, accomplishments at the upper limit of human capability are not the only heroic stories that are told at an Olympic Games. During the Sydney 2000 Games, Equatorial Guinea swimmer Eric 'the eel' Moussambani attained notoriety for his *inability* to swim. Eric had only just learned to swim before coming to the Olympics and crowds cheered him on for completing one length, taking nearly double the time of the slowest other competitor. While it may seem peculiar that someone of such limited swimming ability should have the privilege of becoming an Olympian, his inclusion is an indication of how the Olympic values are applied in the Games, which permit the inclusion of athletes from developing countries where there is a lack of training facilities. Despite Eric's lack of speed, his performance set an Olympic record for his country. Sadly, the IOC President Jacques Rogge disapproved of this incident, leading to questions over the merit of the 'wild card' competition entry system (MacKay 2003). Nevertheless, Olympic history is dotted with similar stories, such as the Jamaican bobsleigh team which had never practised on ice until their competition at the Olympic Winter Games of Calgary 1988, or Eddie 'the eagle' Edwards, the struggling ski jumper from Great Britain who finished last in every jump also at Calgary.

Becoming an Olympian is an entry to a unique community – the World Olympians Association to be precise – and athletes have always been the centre of the Olympic movement's discourse and priorities. Despite Nike's ambush marketing campaign at the Atlanta 1996 Games where they used the slogan 'You Don't Win Silver, You Lose Gold', athletes who did not come first in their contest have also been made heroes by their home nations. Both the experiences of the Jamaican bobsleigh team and Eddie the Eagle have become stories worthy of telling through the medium of feature-length films and this speaks volumes to how being an Olympic athlete is a multi-factorial signifier of excellence, effort and personal achievement.

Of course, this is not to say that all elite athletes are necessarily great role models or worthy of elevation to some higher status. After all, such infamous athletes as Ben Johnson, who was renowned for being caught using steroids after a remarkable victory at the Seoul 1988 100m sprint final, have become symbolic of elite sports that have gone too far in how seriously athletes take their work. Indeed, given the way in which doping tests function today and the rapid progress of performance-enhancing methods, all Olympic athletes may be using undetectable means of performance enhancement, bringing into question what we think we admire when witnessing the performance of an Olympic athlete.

To conclude, these various histories of the Olympic Games reveal the complex context within which they take place, as an entity for which many parts of the world have a strong sense of ownership and political investment. Undoubtedly, today's Olympic community is shaped by the early years of Coubertin's Games for the privileged, but they have also moved with the times along with the rise of the elite sports industries. Our next chapter considers how this trajectory is situated within broader processes of social change, whereby the Olympics have become a defining event through which to project notions of national identity and social priorities.

SOCIETY AND IDENTITY

When a nation bids to host an Olympic Games, the process can be fraught with so many challenges that even winning consensus around the value of bidding can be difficult to achieve. Invariably, concerns are expressed by politicians, the public and the media about the significant amount of public funds that will be necessary to spend on staging the Games, a concern exacerbated by the fact that many previous Games have shown only limited evidence of financial or social benefits arising from the experience. Furthermore, objections are often expressed about the value of hosting a mega-event in a time of financial or political difficulties, where other priorities exist. Indeed, such anxieties arise for any nation that hosts a mega-event of such a scale as an Olympics. In fact, occasionally, the particular local circumstances of a nation can quickly change its ability to deliver the event. Indeed, so wide and diverse are the concerns of domestic interest groups that the process towards the eventual delivery of an Olympic Games can be incredibly fragile and, in some cases, impossible to realize. For instance, the 1908 Games were due to take place in Rome, but because of mounting concerns about the public cost of the Games and the eventual eruption of Mount Vesuvius, they were moved to London (McIntire 2009). Alternatively, the 1976 Winter Games were due to be staged in Denver, but owing to spiraling inflation rates, a grassroots movement succeeded in voting out the Games, whereupon they were moved to Innsbruck (Sanko 1999).

More recently, the construction of venues for the Athens 2004 Olympic Games was so delayed that debates took place within the media about whether the IOC would move the Games elsewhere at the last minute (Whyte 2000), an action that it is able to take should it decide that the host city has not honoured its obligations. In other cases, without overwhelming public support at the bid stage, it may be inconceivable for the IOC to award a city the Games. Both the Toronto 2008 and the Chicago 2016 bids are cases in point, where public opposition is reported to have been a factor in the Games being awarded elsewhere. Yet, perhaps the most well-known examples where national and global circumstances have disrupted the delivery of the Games were around the Berlin 1916, Tokyo and Helsinki 1940 Games,[1] and the London 1944 Games (as well as the Winter Games counterparts) which were each cancelled because of the World Wars. Indeed, these are the only Games that have been cancelled in the history of the modern Olympics so far.

Once the Games are won, the scale of the debate around their value and the scrutiny under which the organizing authorities come reach an unprecedented level. Indeed, public opinion about the value of hosting the Games tends to dip dramatically from just before winning the bid to the weeks leading up to the Games (Cashman and Hughes 1999). Each and every action of the organizing committee and, at times, the activity of the Olympic movement more widely, may be subject to criticism and in need of public justification. For instance, on the approach to the Beijing 2008 Games, the British Olympic Association (BOA) released special guidelines that would govern the conduct of its athletes when in China, mindful of how these Games were being politicized. While the BOA may have intended these guidelines to protect its athletes from commercial or political exploitation, they were discussed in the public sphere as a restriction of British athletes' human rights and, in this context, the Olympic Games were presented as having undermined freedom of speech (Leapman and Powell 2008).

This level of scrutiny over organizers' actions should not surprise us; indeed, it is a crucial dimension of any democratic society. After all, the Olympic Games bring considerable disruption to many national priorities, programmes and infrastructures, which in turn may jeopardize many peoples' lives and this requires justification and transparency of decision-making. However, this level of scrutiny also helpfully articulates why matters of identity and representation are critical to staging an Olympic Games, since there is a considerable amount of public interest invested in their taking place. Thus, at the centre of this interrogation of the Games' social value are questions over ownership, public expectations and whether they represent the interests and concerns of the bidding population and the wider Olympic movement beyond its financial stakeholders.

In this context, the public discourse on the character of the Games and how that intersects with the lived interests of communities that they affect can become central to what takes place over an Olympic hosting period. Moreover, considerations of national and local identity and addressing social priorities often become a pivotal point of debate during the Olympic Games hosting process, where discussions about what kind of Games they ought to be come to the fore. Indeed, since very early on in the history of the modern Games, they have been seen as a vehicle for articulating a nation's identity (Collins 2007, McIntire 2009, Xin 2006). However, beyond symbolic statements, they have also been a gateway to changing the projected identity of a nation by creating 'turning points' in its history. For instance, Miller (1992) and Bridges (2008) discuss how the Seoul 1988 Olympic Games provided a route through which to develop new diplomatic relations for South Korea where previously there were none. These Games also fostered trade agreements that brought the country into the global economy.

The present chapter considers how concerns about social issues and identity have defined the Olympic Games in the past and what this may mean for their future. Initially, we outline some key moments in Olympic history when both planned and unplanned narratives about the Games have been pivotal in how they were perceived and subsequently remembered. Here, we also identify how the IOC has shaped the Olympic persona over the years and the challenge for host cities in aligning themselves with its ideals and expectations. Next, we consider what underpins a city's desire to host an Olympic Games and the challenges over what local and national legacy mega-events can leave behind, a theme we take up further in Chapter 8. It is around this construct that problems begin to arise, as the direction a city may take after hosting an Olympic Games may not suit the aspirations of everyone within its population. Thus, we conclude the chapter by examining aspects of identity that are recurrent sites of resistance around the Olympics, focusing particularly on the tensions between global, corporate and exclusive versus local, community and inclusive policies and processes.

Throughout, we argue that the Olympic Games is a project of identity formation, contestation and consolidation. In other words, it can give rise to new ideas about a population's identity, serve to challenge established ideas, or reinforce clichés and stereotypes. These processes occur concurrently during the hosting period fuelled by personal as well as media-led cultural and political discourses. Sometimes, these ways of constructing identity may articulate serious social issues, which have important consequences for people's perception of the value of the Games, as in the case of debates about forced evictions, where communities are displaced and destroyed to make way for new Olympic venues. Alternatively, the Games' organizers may find a way of intervening in an emerging discourse and transforming it into something else. For example, in the case of the Athens 2004 Games, after months of criticism over their delayed venues, the organizers included a comedic film within the opening ceremony depicting construction workers in the stadium moving around at high speed to finish the stadium just in time for the ceremony (Murphy 2004).[2] This diffused the sense of bad feeling around the criticisms about the stadiums, almost obscuring the importance of what were otherwise seen to be serious circumstances for Greece. Equally, the identity of a nation may be programmed into an Olympic Games' assets via the use of symbols and branding motifs. For instance, for the London 2012 Games, the two mascots associated with the Olympic and Paralympic Games were named after important historical connections between the UK and these Games. Thus, *Wenlock* is the name of the mascot for the Olympic Games, after the Much Wenlock Games, the British contribution to reviving the Olympics in modern times. Alternatively, *Mandeville* is the name of the Paralympic mascot, named after Stoke Mandeville, the village in England which was the birthplace of Paralympic sport.

THE BEST-LAID PLANS OF IOC AND OCOG

In our analysis of Olympic narratives about social issues and identity, we distinguish between *planned* and *unplanned* narratives that emerge around an Olympic hosting period. In both cases, these narratives may derive from either the host nation's population (organizers and public) or the Olympic movement, but each deserves a different form of interpretation and critique. For instance, when during the Munich 1972 Games, Palestinian terrorists struck the Israeli team in the athletes' village, this had obviously nothing to do with what the organizers had intended for their Games. However, it may have spoken to the attitude of the organizers towards security which, some have speculated, was relatively relaxed owing to a deliberate attempt from the German government to overcome the international image of Germany's past as a totalitarian nation. Nevertheless, the attacks became the defining story of the Games, a clear example of an unplanned narrative that had important consequences for host identity perceptions for many years to come. In contrast, when North and South Korean athletes marched together for the first time at the opening ceremony of the Sydney 2000 Games, this gesture of unity was the result of considerable planning and investment on behalf of the IOC and other organizations. As such, it may be seen as part of the broader IOC intentions for the Olympic movement to bring about progress towards peace and reconciliation and make this central to the Games' narrative.

As suggested above, *unplanned* narratives are those that arise during the process of hosting a Games without forewarning or prior strategic development, but which then become part of a host city's or international audience's core understanding of what has been important about an Olympic Games. A good example of this occurred at the Salt Lake City 2002 Games, which took place just five months after the New York 9/11 terrorist attack. In the lead-up to the Games, the Salt Lake Organizing Committee sought to utilize the iconic, tattered flag from the destroyed World Trade Centre site within the opening ceremony's Athletes Parade. As Salt Lake City 2002 CEO Mitt Romney (2004) recounts, the IOC resisted this, arguing that the 'Olympic Charter stipulated that displays of nationalistic sentiment were not permitted'. After discussion the IOC accepted its utilization within the ceremony, as the flag that would be raised during the US National Anthem (Harvey and Abrahamson 2002). Yet, because of its fragile state, this was not an option. In the end, the IOC agreed to its use elsewhere within the ceremony, though its particular location within the order of proceedings was paramount, when trying to understand whether or not this decision compromised the neutral position of the Olympic protocol. As Romney says, the flag was 'brought into the stadium just before the anthem was played and held in front of the symphony and choir' (2004: 352). This decision located the flag's presence somewhere between the cultural elements and the official protocol, thus allowing the Olympic movement to acknowledge the tragedy that had beset the USA and the importance of the flag for national morale, without contravening its rules. As IOC member for the USA Anita DeFrantz said after this concession had been made: 'The Olympic movement around the world has expressed its sympathy for the victims of September 11th in many ways since that tragic day. Showing the flag in this respect is just one more way' (DeFrantz, cited in Atkinson and Young 2002: 63). This example reveals how domestic histories can often be crucial in making aspects of a Games memorable for both a local and global audience. One may even argue that such ceremonies require powerful symbols, in order to demonstrate the values of a nation. Moreover, they are powerful ways to draw in emotive journalistic expressions, which Zelizer and Allen (2002) have argued prioritize the elevation of 'trauma' stories since 9/11. At the Beijing 2008 opening ceremony, a similar narrative occurred, as a child survivor from the May 2008 Sichuan earthquake accompanied celebrated Chinese basketball star Yao Ming in leading the Chinese athlete delegation in the parade of nations.

Unforeseen moments of patriotism are very different from the way in which certain stories are pre-*planned* by an Organizing Committee, political party, media organization or, indeed, from the recurrent anti-Olympic, anti-corporate resistance that occurs around each Games. For instance, at the Sydney 2000 Olympic Games, the final five bearers of the Olympic torch were all women, which was treated as a statement about the importance given by Sydney to female participation at the Olympics. This decision was also taken in the context of the 100-year anniversary of the first women to take part in an Olympic Games. This example shows how a nation can deliberately associate itself with certain social values that it may wish to champion, in order to make a statement about its national values. By implication it also reveals why an OCOG may be subject to criticism, if it fails to represent certain interests in the staging of the Games.

Alternatively, an OCOG can be caught unaware in situations when its own planned narratives about its Games are transformed as a result of unplanned events. For example, the Beijing 2008 Games organizers asserted the role of Beijing's population as part of its core value statement: 'Green Olympics, High-Tech Olympics, People's Olympics' (BOCOG 2008b). However, a series of events leading up to the Games would make a mockery of elements of this slogan, particularly the emphasis on the 'people'. Protests around the torch relay by human rights activists highlighted China's neglect for the people – or humanity generally – within its Games. Moreover, the Chinese artist Ai Weiwei resigned from his role as Olympic stadium adviser and US film director Steven Spielberg did the same for his consultancy role in the opening ceremony preparations, both of them motivated by perceived contradictions within the Beijing Games' hosting process. In these cases, the planned narrative about Beijing 2008 was hijacked by campaigners to articulate a more controversial and newsworthy counterpoint. BOCOG could hardly have foreseen how this turn of events would dominate the international impression of its Games, even though there were warning signs about how China's domestic human rights laws were being received by the international community (Adi and Miah 2011). Thus, here is an example of how unplanned narratives can surprise Olympic organizers and dominate the media debates about what was historically important about any particular Olympic Games.

THE OLYMPIC PERSONA

A further challenge involved with hosting an Olympic Games is that the host city and nation must accept the 'Olympic transaction' (Cha 2010: 2360), whereby it aligns itself with a number of dimensions of the Olympic identity, which may have little to do with how a city's population sees itself, or how it appears to visitors. These dimensions are often expressed as the 'values of Olympism' (IOC 2010a), which emerge in different forms through Olympic documentation and rhetoric. For example, the IOC website section on 'Olympism in action', lists three values: 'excellence', 'respect' and 'friendship', and six areas of action: 'sport for all', 'development through sport', 'education through sport', 'women and sport', 'peace through sport', and 'sport and the environment'. Elsewhere, the Olympic Charter emphasizes the value of 'fair play' as a key dimension of the Olympics, along with such concepts as 'non-discrimination' and 'human dignity'. The reason for these different discourses on the Olympic identity is that Olympism is a fluid philosophical perspective. Its roots lay in Coubertin's vision, but even this was not singular or complete when the IOC first convened in 1894. Rather, Coubertin developed the philosophy of Olympism over his lifetime and it has, ever since, continued to evolve through the interpretation of those who have had the responsibility for steering the Olympic movement from one Olympiad to the next. Indeed, as we noted in the previous chapter, for many years, the official IOC history of the rings associated each of them with a specific continent, a view that is now regarded as unsupported by evidence.

Thus, even the official view of what the Olympic values express has been subject to changes of understanding and emphasis over the years. A further dimension of this is that ideas are often simplified for the purpose of marketing, which may undermine their philosophical complexity. This is most apparent within the IOC 'tool kits' for OCOGs and the Olympic family, but also in the advertising campaigns developed to promote Olympism. Notably, the IOC's 'Celebrate Humanity' and 'The Best of Us' campaigns are each examples of how the philosophy of Olympism is transformed into a set of marketing ideas, which aim to express something very precise about the Olympic movement, but equally may be interpreted in quite different ways depending on the audience (Maguire et al. 2008). The IOC expects to portray the universal values of 'excellence, friendship and respect' through these campaigns. Yet Barnard et al. (2006) claim that the celebration of 'humanity' conflicts with the way the Games remain deeply rooted in national discourses, thus demonstrating the endurance of the nation as a rhetorical and ideological presence (ibid. 50) which the Games still rely on to secure strong support and following, rather than true advancement towards open international and intercultural exchanges.

The appropriation of these Olympic values is essential to the successful staging of the Games, but it may require considerable political rhetoric to convince a host nation population of their value. Indeed, the practical implications of this can be challenging, as many aspects of society will most likely feel very little affinity with the values of Olympism or see much cause to align their institution's own values with these Olympic ideals. Indeed, there may even be a deep resentment of the way in which sport, as a cultural form, has courted transnational corporations in support of its endeavours. To this end, some potential local Games stakeholders may regard the elevation of Olympic values within host city rhetoric as disingenuous, concealing more important, implicit Olympic agendas such as protecting the interests of its corporate partners.

In sum, given that an Olympic Games is unlikely to happen in a country more frequently than once every fifty years, questions about how an Organizing Committee should articulate the identity of a city, region or nation are extremely sensitive and controversial. Aspects of identity are implied within all dimensions of the Games and their negotiation becomes a fusion of the host city population's sense of self in combination with the Olympic values. Organizers must resign themselves to the fact that the Games will be read by audiences in these terms. For example, the fact that the Sydney 2000 opening ceremony began with an Aboriginal welcome, followed by the dance of a young Caucasian girl, was read as a statement about the positioning of these populations within Australia. To this end, one may ask why the pursuit of Olympic host city status interests city leaders at all, given how divisive it may be to undertake this role. The answer to this question has to do with the long-term aspirations of a city's leaders to advance economic agendas in terms of global trade development or sustaining a world leading position, as the next section articulates.

BECOMING A WORLD CITY

Over the last few decades, one dominant preoccupation of the Games' host organizers is to ensure that the staging of the event has an impact on how the host city is perceived in the global sphere and, in particular, that the process leads to its being recognized as a world-class city. Such aspirations apply to such diverse places as Barcelona in 1992, Mexico City in 1968, Seoul in 1988 or Beijing in 2008. Mega-events like the Olympic Games are particularly effective platforms to achieve this transformation into world-city status, accelerating a process that may otherwise take significantly longer to achieve. Burbank et al. (2001) discuss this trend by noting that events such as the Olympic Games make ideal vehicles for cities to pursue growth, as they provide access to a 'symbolic regime' (ibid. 26). In turn, this allows 'growth proponents access to the popular symbolism of international sports and makes opposition to development projects associated with those symbols more difficult' (ibid. 28) than with other kinds of project.

Yet, there is considerable disagreement about what it means to be a world-class city or how one may qualify such an achievement. Paul (2004) identifies various bodies of literature that include such indicators as the presence of transnational corporation headquarters, banking and financial institutions, producer services, or the hosting of global spectacles. He goes on to note that more recent studies look instead at 'external relations and flows between world cities' (ibid. 572), but notes the uncertainty of what might be the moment when a city can claim this status: 'Does a new sports stadium make one's city "international" or "world-class"? A mass transit system? An international cultural festival? A world trade center?' (ibid.). Florida (2004) argues that one can measure the status of a city most effectively by examining its creative economy and ecology or, more specifically, its ability to nurture and retain a 'creative class'. This thesis challenges other indicators of achievement, but it still begs further questions about what makes a place world class. Is this about having world-class facilities, such as sports venues, or being a world leader for promoting gender equality? Clearly, interpretations of what it might mean to be world class could be quite diverse.

Given the above ambiguities, the Olympic Games are often seen as a useful aid in the pursuit of 'world class' status because they represent a globally renowned brand (see also Chapter 6). In many cases, the Olympic Games have proved to be a catapult for a city's international profile, leading to increased levels of tourism, greater economic investment and stronger connections with other world cities. Those cities that already have a strong history as an economic or cultural centre may apply to host the Games in order to consolidate their role as a powerful economic base or as a centre of cultural excellence. Indeed, the pursuit of hosting a Games is often predicated on the expected 'impact' it will have on selected cultural, social and economic indicators, as we discuss in Chapter 8. Regardless of whether the city can claim world-class status – or indeed whether this claim can be sustained beyond the Games period – the assertion that city leaders can create an opportunity to reinvent local identity and enhance its prospects is crucial to explaining why cities bid to host the Olympics (Verdaguer 1995). Indeed, hosting the Olympic Games is often championed as a mechanism for reinventing a city.

OWNING THE OLYMPICS[3]

The remainder of this chapter addresses how identity has been negotiated through debates around a number of social concerns at previous Games. We argue that the modern Olympic Games are defined by a number of recurring themes, all of which speak to the identity of a host city and nation. In particular, we identify areas of tension that provide an insight into the complex identity politics of the Olympic proposition. These are neatly summarized in the often overlapping dichotomy between the emphasis on global, corporate and exclusive processes versus local, community-led and inclusive obligations of Games organizers. At the heart of these oppositions are questions about ownership of the Olympic programme and narrative – both the Games and the movement – in social, cultural and economic terms. There is no neat mapping of these concepts as oppositional to each other. For example, corporate interests can be both local and global in the context of the Games, as the IOC-led Olympic sponsorship programme addresses the interests of the transnational partners who contribute to funding various Games editions, while respective OCOGs must also secure local commercial partners. However, for simplicity we will focus the conversation around their differences, which helpfully reveal why identity is in tension around an Olympic Games and how it is crucial to negotiate potential contradictions effectively to ensure the Games lead to sustainable and meaningful legacies and, above all, can respond to the concerns of local communities.

GLOBAL VERSUS LOCAL

The global identity of the Olympics has been central to its modern revival and, as we suggest in Chapter 1, helps to explain why Coubertin's revival was successful. Thus, the Olympic Games may help to foster global cooperation and intercultural exchanges. For example, the Olympic Solidarity programme, explained in more detail in Chapter 6, is one important way in which the Olympic movement makes a commitment to addressing global inequalities in sport and attempts to level the playing field. In this respect, the global character of the Games is also its strength. Yet, Maguire (1999) notes that the promotion of global values may lead to disenchantment within local communities, provoking an 'ethnically assertive and defensive nationalism' (p. 187). Indeed, this may be to the broader detriment of global cultural, political and economic flows. In the Olympic context, this explains why it is common to find moments of strong nationalist expression within host city narratives, since the Games provide an opportunity for communities to re-encounter nationhood in a peaceful and collective manner.

Thus, the Olympic Games expose moments of tension between expressions of local and global identity. While in the bid stage – and often at the presentation of the bid to the IOC – global values are elevated by drawing attention to the diversity of nations that exist within a bid city; once the Games are awarded, the hosting process tends to privilege attention to expressions of local issues, identity and interest. However, concerns over these tensions may not be heard by organizers because of the dominance of the global context of the Games. The Salt Lake City 2002 Olympic Winter Games are a case in point, where the local community was characterized by the global media in terms of its Mormon religion, with its attitudes to marriage and alcohol consumption occupying the interests of journalists (Gerlach 2002). Despite local laws prohibiting the consumption of alcohol in public places, one of the major public squares within the host city during Games time was sponsored by the alcoholic beverage company Budweiser, the association with which was articulated via a giant inflatable bottle of beer and visible branding of 'Bud World'. The square where this occurred was located barely two blocks away from Temple Square, a landmark for the city's Mormon community, which advocates sobriety. Placing an alcoholic sponsor's event in a city where a significant proportion of its residents do not drink alcohol and where public restaurants cannot serve alcohol indicates that, as in so many event hosting processes, local sensitivities are often neither fully explored nor all local groups fully consulted about their preferences and thoughts in how the city celebrates its mega-event. Of course, identifying who is at fault around such examples is not at all clear and, in this particular case, it was the local city stakeholders, rather than the international requirements of the Olympic movement, that led to this situation. After all, Budweiser was a domestic rather than global IOC sponsor. It would also be wrong to suggest that this decision upset everyone within the local population, given that there are non-Mormon communities in Salt Lake City and the Games were also representing the broader US population. However, it is examples like this that explain how the Olympics shine a light on the tensions that exist within local communities over the identity and culture of a place and the way the Games balance representation of local, national and international interests.

As the 'Bud World' example illustrates, the Olympic Games can be an alienating event for some communities whose values do not align with the needs of the Olympic organizers. The Games require a city's population to adopt and integrate the values associated with them, rather than acting as an event that is born out of place-specific community values. In one sense, hosting the Olympic Games ought to lend itself to developing synergies with many other identities, as its elevation of 'friendship' and 'non-discrimination' as primary values is reasonably universal. Indeed, this is an important reason to consider why it is that the Olympic Games can sustain such levels of collective and unified support from one city to the next. Yet, the practical implementation of these values into a host city programme reveals tensions in how they are applied and made sense of by people with different perspectives. In principle, the broad liberal values of the Olympic movement allow for the creation of a unified community – consolidated by the celebration of sport, culture and the environment, the three dimensions of Olympism (IOC 2002a). In practice, the Olympic Games deals in global values that are only relevant to local communities in abstract terms, and may fail to reflect their particularities. The consequence is an event that is often valued by the organizers more for its financial benefits than for its universal ideals.

EXCLUSIVE VERSUS INCLUSIVE

There are various ways in which the Olympics engender the belief that they benefit only a few privileged people. Becoming an Olympian provides access to an exclusive community of people who have enjoyed a certain kind of success. Here, the exclusivity is acknowledged and valued because there is an assumption that it is based on merit. However, the exclusivity of the Games goes further than this. An obvious starting point is the bid for the Games, whereby there can be only one winner and several losers who will have invested considerable time and money into competing for the Games. Once the Games are awarded, there is competition between sports fans over a limited number of tickets for official events, which leads unavoidably to many disappointed people. Here again, the global and local divide occurs and it is common for host nation journalists to complain about the fact that an unreasonable number of tickets are reserved for sale in other countries, while millions of host nationals who pay for the Games through taxation are not able to obtain a single ticket for the sports events. Furthermore, even if one is able to secure a ticket, getting to the Olympic Games is also a financial and logistical challenge. The price of accommodation in the host city rises considerably during the Olympic Games, making a stay unaffordable for many people and even more so for those who come from abroad. It is such circumstances that lead critics to argue that experiencing the Olympic Games first hand is essentially for the privileged few. Finally, at the organizational level, Olympic sponsorship is based on 'exclusive' contracts, which maximize the value of the investment by the chosen commercial partners, but also imply that many other organizations cannot benefit from the Games association. This speaks to the utilization of the Olympic identity or rather, the Olympic rings as a global brand, which is fiercely protected by the IOC to ensure the commercial interests of its stakeholders are safe.

In this sense, the Games both welcome the world and want everyone involved, and yet operate as an exclusive brand. All the same, the hosting process requires adherence to certain principles of inclusivity and public accountability, which have resulted in a range of initiatives to address these tensions. For example, the London 2012 Organizing Committee made national *inclusion* a priority within its programme by introducing a distinct 'Inspired by London 2012' brand, which allowed a wide range of organizations from around the UK to associate their projects with the London 2012 visual identity, without jeopardizing the rights of global sponsors to exclusive commercial association with the Olympic rings. This was achieved by creating a distinct emblem, which drew on the format of the London 2012 emblem design, but which did not include the Olympic rings. Achieving collaboration across the entire Games programme (which includes cultural activity, educational programmes, the sports competitions, etc.) while maintaining freedom to pursue projects in an organic way, as took place through London's Inspired brand, is one of the principal challenges of an organizing committee in maximizing the inclusivity of an Olympic programme.

Concerns about exclusion are manifested in various ways at the Games, but most strikingly in the form of disaffected communities or interest groups. The Sydney 2000 bid documents put a clear emphasis on the visibility that Aboriginal people and multicultural communities would have during the staging of the Games, in particular through the Olympic cultural programme (Hanna 1999, McGeoch and Korporaal 1994, Sydney Bid Ltd 1992). Arguably, this was one fact that influenced the decision of the IOC to award the Games to Sydney, as it conveyed how Sydney 2000 would be a route towards reconciliation, which aligns with one of the IOC's core interests for the Games. However, at the time of staging the event, many groups – ethnic minority communities in particular – were not given the chance to contribute effectively in the decision-making for cultural programming (Multicultural Arts Alliance 1999). Their involvement in the preparations for the sporting programme was even less apparent. Following the promises made at the bid stage, an Aboriginal Commission and a Multicultural Commission were created within the Sydney Organizing Committee for the Olympic Games (SOCOG) but their role was merely advisory and poorly adjusted to the changeable agendas of the decision-makers (García 2010).

In particular, there were disputes over the primary site for the Games – Homebush Bay – which was one area with a contested land claim. This became an important symbol for how the interests of Aboriginal people had been neglected around the

Games, and drew attention to the ongoing anxieties about integration and governmental responsibility. Indeed, for some years, campaigners had sought a governmental apology for the treatment of the Aboriginal community and this campaign became visible nationally as well as internationally on the build up to the Games. To this end, the decision to award the cauldron-lighting privilege to Cathy Freeman had special symbolic value for Australians. To international viewers of the ceremony, she may be unknown beyond her sporting accomplishments, but in this moment of national prestige, Freeman became a symbol for Australian values and Aborigine identity. Freeman also became a symbol of women's participation in the Games, which was reinforced by the choice of women as all five final Sydney torch relay runners. This narrative was not only representative of host city values but also aligned with ongoing Olympic movement priorities regarding the promotion of women in sport (Henry et al. 2004, Henry and Robinson 2010).

Highlighting national identity tensions is another recurrent theme from Games to Games. At the Vancouver 2010 Games, the Organizing Committee created a 'four host nations' programme to promote shared ownership of the Games over the Olympic period. This involved an extensive cultural programme overseen by leading representatives of the various indigenous communities of the host region, British Columbia. Alternatively, at the Barcelona 1992 Games, it was the dichotomy between Spanish national identity and Catalan regional identity which captured global narratives about the city's positioning in contemporary Spain and resulted in all the official Games activities being presented in four official languages, including Catalan. In the lead-up to London 2012, discussion has also arisen about what it means to be British in present times and how devolved nations such as Scotland, as well as Northern Ireland and Wales, relate to England in the Games context. These examples reveal how the Olympic Games can be a catalyst for the renegotiation of ongoing identity concerns. Each of them has provoked public discussion about the boundaries of nationhood and, more broadly, whose identity is represented in the staging of a unique national event. This is what makes every decision of an Olympic organizing committee particularly vulnerable to public criticism, since building a narrative of the Games that is inclusive of as wide a range of voices as possible brings to the fore many of the fundamental beliefs or anxieties that exist within a country.

CORPORATE VERSUS COMMUNITY

Identity conflicts and social concerns also emerge around the values propagated by the Olympic movement in its pursuit of economic stability. For, while the Olympic Charter elevates the values of friendship, respect and excellence, it is transnational corporate investments that make the Games possible and, by implication, influence the movement's priorities. One such recurrent bargain that often causes public outrage is the allocation of large amounts of Olympic tickets – either for their staff or for their guests – to global sponsors such as Coca-Cola or McDonalds. Given the limited number of tickets and the fact that only a fraction of the people who apply for tickets will get them, this corporatization of the Games' most privileged assets is at odds with the democratizing principles Olympism aspires to promote. The anger this may generate is exacerbated when the television coverage of the sports reveals row after row of empty seats, because those with free tickets may choose not to use them and often fail to redistribute them.

However, much more serious than ticket allocations is the wholesale commercialization of the Olympic Games by corporate partners. Perhaps the most profound example of this was the Atlanta 1996 Games, labelled by historians as the 'Coca-Cola Games' in reference to the fact that Atlanta is Coca-Cola's global headquarters and that the company has been an Olympic partner since 1928. Yet, the name also befits an Olympic Games edition that was funded entirely by private bodies, with significant funds from Coca-Cola itself, rather than having any governmental financial stakeholder. The consequence of these over-commercialized Games was a failure to deliver important logistical services that require city-wide cooperation and traditionally rely on public investment, such as transport. In turn, this led to the IOC's discouragement of this model and eventually to a change in the host city contract, which now stipulates that host city governmental stakeholders must share the financial burden of the Games (Preuss 2006).

A further level up the scale of severity of how detrimental corporate interests may be to community interests at an Olympics is the way in which the pursuit of the Olympic 'Grand project' (Sinclair 2011) leads to the creation of displaced communities, often via what some call 'forced evictions'. Again, this is a recurrent theme within the Olympic Games hosting process, as city planners draw boundaries around the spaces required to stage the Games. Concerns about forced evictions have arisen in the most recent Games editions. In Beijing 2008, the destruction of some of the city's traditional neighbourhoods (hutongs) and their subsequent rebuilding and gentrification involved the removal of established communities. Also, for the Barcelona 1992 Games, centrally located 'barrios' were demolished to make way for the Olympic Village, which subsequently became a new city neighbourhood retaining the name of *Villa Olimpica*. Alternatively, the impact of an Olympic Games on a city's local housing policy can mean the neglect of its homeless population, who struggle to find their needs addressed during the Games period. This was made most prominent during the Vancouver 2010 Games with the creation by grassroots communities of the self-proclaimed Olympic Tent Village, an area that was created and inhabited by the city's homeless population in part to foreground their having been neglected by the city during the Olympiad. Finally, just a few months after Rio de Janeiro won the rights to the 2016 Olympic Summer Games, stories emerged about how the so-called 'favelas' may be demolished to make way for the Games. This prompted the United Nations Housing Rapporteur to express concerns about progress towards the 2016 Games (United Nations 2011). In these cases, it is the perceived commercial value of Olympic land that exacerbates the marginalization of local community interests.

Finally, the tension between corporate interests and community values is often articulated by subtle but crucial interventions from the Olympic commercial partners which, in the case of sponsors, aim to locate their products within new demographic communities or, in the case of broadcasters, aim to ensure maximum audience outreach. For example, Nauright and Magdalinski (2000) discuss how the Olympic food services provider McDonalds has 'corporatized' the school classroom via Olympic educational packs, complete with branded merchandise. In such cases, the dual process of providing a service for the Olympic movement while at the same time developing brand loyalty towards a sponsor via the education system may be seen as the ultimate corruption of Olympic ideals and is a most profound symbol of how Olympism can be usurped by corporate interests. Another type of imposition has been discussed in the context of how the interests of television broadcasters have led to the changing of Olympic sports schedules to the neglect of the primary stakeholder in the Games – the athletes. For instance, in the lead-up to the Beijing 2008 Games, NBCUniversal forced the change of schedule for the swimming finals, in order to suit their audiences (Campbell 2006). We discuss the implications of this in more detail in Chapter 7.

In conclusion, when examining the last century of the Olympic Games, there are clear, recurrent themes that show how the construction of identity is of central importance to Olympic hosts and the Olympic movement generally. These stories also reveal how identity is not a fixed construct, but becomes manifest through a series of struggles. A good example of this is the protest by Tommie Smith and John Carlos, the US athletes at the Mexico City 1968 Games, who utilized their position on the winners' podium to demonstrate their support for American civil rights (Hartmann 1996). While their actions were criticized, they became symbolic of a shift that was about to take place within the USA, becoming a dominant viewpoint on race relations that would shape the next four decades. Sometimes, a mega-event like the Olympics can become the subject of controversy just because its pursuit is seen to conflict with other, more deeply held values. Indeed, the pursuit of 'world class' status that the Olympic Games engender may involve radical transformations to local communities, which may not be welcome. Understanding the long-term implications of how a mega-event can affect the culture of a city is very difficult, but it almost certainly means the introduction of greater security measures and narrow commercial monopolies, which can neglect other ways of organizing societies.

By considering these themes, we are able to glimpse how the Olympics have been a catalyst for debate about some of the most important social concerns of the twentieth century. Thus, paying attention to identity, representation and potential social injustices that may arise from hosting a Games is crucial to their staging, not least because the widespread public support a bid requires to be successful will depend on commitments to these matters. However, perhaps more importantly, identity issues become crucial because the process towards becoming an Olympic city involves an alignment of values from both the Olympic movement and the host nation. Thus, the host population must make sense of the Olympic values and symbols and, in turn, the Olympics must become part of a city's identity and history. This is particularly challenging given that the Olympic movement courts relationships with large transnational corporations as well as being heavily involved in work with developing nations. Nevertheless, this negotiation underpins the relationship that evolves around an Olympic Games between the host and the Olympic movement and their compatibility becomes an influential part of securing local and international support. In short, it is necessary to persuade members of the IOC that the next Olympics deserve to be hosted in a given city and, in turn, convince the public that they should accept the enormous inconvenience that the Games will bring in exchange for the potential legacy benefits.

CULTURE AND EDUCATION

NOT JUST A SPORTS EVENT

As Chapter 1 indicates, Pierre de Coubertin's vision for Olympism was for it to become a broad, far-reaching 'philosophy of life', of which an integral part should be the pursuit and celebration of other human endeavours, *not* just sport. Indeed, the first 'Fundamental Principle' of the Olympic Charter stipulates that Olympism blends 'sport with culture and education', seeking 'to create a way of life based on the joy of effort, the educational value of good example and respect for universal fundamental ethical principles' (IOC 2010a). This alerts us to the idea that, while the Olympic Games is often regarded to be the most important sports event in the calendar, it should also be a vehicle for cultural expression and educational development. Indeed, it reveals that this commitment is as much a part of the Olympic programme as the sports events themselves. A requirement to host a cultural programme is even built into the host city contract. For example, in the case of London 2012, the contract states:

> The OCOG must organize a programme of cultural events which shall be submitted to the IOC for its prior written approval not later than three years before the Games. This programme must serve to promote

harmonious relations, mutual understanding and friendship among the participants and other persons attending the Games. The cultural programme must cover at least the entire period during which the Olympic Village is open. The cultural programme shall also include the IOC's own programme of exhibitions, if any. Part of the seating area for the events on the cultural programme taking place in the City must be reserved by the OCOG, free of charge, for the participants accredited at the Games. The OCOG shall ensure that sponsorship, promotional, advertising and broadcasting rights relating to the cultural programme are not granted to competitors of the Olympic sponsors and broadcasters.

(IOC 2005a: 18)

However, in contrast with other Games programmes, there are no technical manuals for culture and the Olympic Charter does not specify how these commitments should be made manifest. This creates a challenge for both an OCOG and the IOC. In the case of the former, local organizers are left uncertain about how much investment in cultural and educational activity is expected by the IOC, while the latter must find a way of making culture and education part of the Games programme without jeopardizing the local host's ability to deliver safe and efficient sport competitions.

One of the explanations for this lack of precision is that the terminology used within the Charter is open to interpretation, with the concepts of sport, culture and education being very broad categories. Additionally, there are philosophical challenges in the use of these three concepts. Thus, sports may be seen as cultural manifestations and educational practices in themselves and as vehicles for understanding the body and for creating new leisure-based, social configurations. As Coubertin says,

Sport must be regarded as a producer of art and an occasion of art. It produces beauty because it gives us the athlete who is a living sculpture. It is an occasion of beauty through the buildings constructed for it, and through the entertainment and festivals that it generates.

(Coubertin, cited in IOC 2002a)

Alternatively, cultural activity – for instance, an art exhibition of sports photography – can be understood as an educational and intellectual endeavour, or as a way of making sense of sport's role in society. This problem of definition and boundaries between these three concepts is made apparent in the report of the IOC 2000 Reform Commission, which, upon recommending investment from the IOC in culture, states that:

> The IOC 2000 Commission understands *culture* inclusively, as all the symbolic forms that make life meaningful for human societies, and further believes that continuing Olympic education is a matter of concern for all members of the Olympic Movement, including IOC members.
>
> (IOC 1999: 17)

Despite the lack of strict guidelines, the implementation of cultural and educational activities has taken on quite precise characteristics and Coubertin's vision sets some precedents for their operationalization. To help explain their application in the modern Olympic context, we know that Coubertin's vision distinguished between sport and athletics, the latter of which he considered to be more closely aligned with his vision for how the Olympics could foster the 'perfect human'. Thus, sports were merely one aspect of this development, though of course they have become the locus of activity for the Olympic movement. It is also apparent that Coubertin wanted the Olympic Games to champion *artistic* excellence, as a form of cultural expression distinct from sport. Indeed, early instances of the Games included arts competitions, as well as sports contests. Thus, artists contributed works of literature, visual art, architecture, performing arts and music all competing for medals in parallel to the athletes. Moreover, the medal winners were originally supposed to make defining contributions for the Games, from becoming the official design for the Olympic stadium (architecture) to the defining Olympic musical composition.

While this aspect of the Games no longer exists in such a form, art and culture remain a core part of the Olympic experience and it would be untrue to say that competitions, of a sort, no longer take place in these disciplines. Indeed, at the Beijing 2008 Olympic Games, there was an Olympic Fine Arts exhibition, which was one of the highest-profile cultural events of the Games, attended by both former IOC President Juan Antonio Samaranch and current President Jacques Rogge, and which had involved a competitive selection process of international artworks. More generally, the

Olympic Games involves a series of creative competitions – though of an admittedly slightly different fashion – to design certain elements of the Games, from public art installations, to venue architecture, to the OCOG emblem, Olympic torch and graphic design components of a Games. Nevertheless, there is no formal awarding of Olympic medals for these types of competitions. Instead, as noted earlier, Olympic cities are required by the IOC to produce a cultural programme of some kind, the guidelines for which have remained loose in contrast with the tight regulations and extensive support manuals that exist for other Olympic components. As a result, OCOGs have often struggled to retain the cultural programme as a high delivery priority compared with other well-known (and closely supervised) Olympic programmes, and the general public has remained largely unaware of this dimension of the Games.

As well as having a strong cultural and artistic undercurrent, Coubertin's original vision was also intimately tied to pedagogic progress and, as Chapter 1 explained, the principles of Olympism were forged through the philosophy of educational institutions. Coubertin himself was an educator. In present times, this commitment is implemented through extensive educational exchanges between schools to develop an understanding of Olympism, a process that tends to take place under the supervision of National Olympic Academies or, in their absence, the NOCs. However, the continuity of such programmes is quite uneven around the world and, while some countries have created long-term commitments to pursuing Coubertin's vision, or a contemporary version of what has been termed Olympic education initiatives, most countries tend to limit activities to the periods leading up to specific Games editions in coordination with respective OCOGs. Indeed, OCOGs have varied in their level of dedication to the education programme and their capacity to make it visible and relevant to Games audiences and related stakeholders.

Despite these challenges, the education and cultural programmes remain critical cornerstones of official Olympic principles and values. As such, one should view the Games as a cultural festival and a platform for educational reform, within which the sports competitions are only one dimension. On this basis, we next consider some of the critical developments in cultural and educational programming around the Games and emerging opportunities in view of the growing demand for the Games to be both sustainable and community-led. We begin by outlining some of the key mechanisms for cultural expression in the Olympic Games programme, before discussing examples of cultural artefacts that have been as historically relevant as the breaking of world records. The chapter concludes with an overview of the Olympic educational infrastructure, which reveals how scholarship and intellectual inquiry provide a crucial foundation for the Olympic movement.

FROM ARTS COMPETITIONS TO CULTURAL OLYMPIADS

There are a variety of places where one may begin to outline the range of cultural activities that take place during an Olympic Games, but perhaps the most useful starting point is to acknowledge the range of ways in which cultural activity is programmed by the OCOG. The primary route towards Olympic cultural programming is the Cultural Olympiad, which is one of the IOC's protected terms and may be used only by the OCOG to articulate its core cultural programme. While this is not the only form of Olympic cultural activity that takes place during a Games, its central position within the OCOG gives it an unrivalled presence within the Olympic programme. The concept of a Cultural Olympiad has a relatively short history, being utilized formally by OCOGs since the Barcelona 1992 Games edition, which launched the notion of a four-year programme (an Olympiad) of cultural activity, starting at the end of the previous Games. Before this, the cultural programme had been officially defined as the Olympic Art Competitions (1912–48), Olympic Art Exhibitions or Olympic Art Festivals.

Coubertin's vision for the Olympic Art Competition was presented formally at a special congress in Paris in 1906 with the first official programme being presented during the Stockholm 1912 Games. These competitions were also named the 'Pentathlon of the Muses', as their purpose was to bring artists to present their work and compete for 'art' medals across five categories: architecture, music, literature, sculpture and painting (see Stanton 2000). The main vision underpinning the initiative was to ensure that the Games acted as a platform to bring together different dimensions of human excellence and ensure that athletes and intellectuals could be mutually inspired. The Pentathlon of the Muses or Art Competitions developed in parallel to other dimensions of the Olympic pageant and provided an avenue for artists to make a direct contribution to the Games. However, the decision to present the work in a competitive fashion was difficult to implement, particularly as there was growing disagreement about how to define categories and how to determine the purpose of eligible 'Olympic art'. Ongoing discussions concerned whether it was necessary to favour explicit or figurative representations of sport as opposed to allowing more abstract manifestations in tune with international arts trends and irrespective of their link to the Olympic theme. A parallel discussion was the adequacy of retaining the established five categories to account for the wealth and diversity of artistic expression, particularly given the growing international outreach of the Games and the subsequent challenge to Western artistic canons as the only possible point of reference. For instance, within the literature section, it was unclear how one would judge and compare a British theatre play with Japanese haikus (poetry form).

The Berlin 1936 Games presented one of the most ambitious examples of an Olympic art programme in this first period. The Games had been clearly identified by the local host as an opportunity to promote the ideals of Nazi Germany and cultural activity was also seen as an excellent vehicle to represent the supremacy of the Arian race and Western civilisation. Cultural innovations brought in at the Berlin Games included the first Olympic torch relay – travelling from Olympia in Greece to the Berlin stadium – and the first artist-led Olympic film, Leni Riefenstahl's *Olympia*. As Payne (2006) recalls:

> Goebbels saw the propaganda potential of an Olympic film and provided Riefenstahl with unprecedented resources. She travelled to Berlin with 30 cameras and hundreds of staff, shot over 400,000 metres of film (over 248 miles), around 250 hours – probably the largest amount of film shot at the time. The subsequent editing took more than 18 months. Olympia was a lavish hymn to sporting prowess and physical beauty and strength, and premiered in 1938 on Hitler's 49th birthday, with the Nazi leader attending as guest of honour.
>
> (Payne 2006: 134)

These cultural manifestations became as central to the Olympic experience as the sports competitions, both taking place during Games time in their symbolic reconstruction for decades to come. From a cultural programming point of view, the most interesting aspect of this particular experience is the evidence that the Games were used as a mechanism to make Germany's national cultural policy discourse more visible internationally, and the use of artistic expression as a platform to contextualize the Games and use them for propaganda purposes, far beyond simple sport representation.

However, by the early 1950s the IOC was strongly divided on the value and purpose of the art competitions and in 1952 it was finally decided to replace the principle of 'Art Competitions' by 'Exhibitions and Festivals'. Beyond the ongoing discussion about actual content, the ultimate reason for the demise of arts competitions was the concern of then IOC President, Avery Brundage, that artists were considered 'professionals' in their undertaking, while sport competitors at the time were strictly 'amateurs' and any athletes who sought commercial gain were refused entry to the Olympic Games.

This new stage in the Olympic cultural programme brought opportunities as well as challenges. On the one hand, Games organizers had greater freedom to define the purpose of such programmes and determine who should be presenting what type of work. On the other, eliminating its competitive nature led to their being divorced from a strong national delegation following and this situation often led to fewer Olympic participants, less audience engagement, and less international focus and visibility. The programme was now mainly a platform for local cultural representation directed according to the specific interests of the host authorities, with much less direct involvement and regulation from the IOC and related global Olympic structures (see García 2008).

Some Olympic host countries saw the programme as an important opportunity to make a statement about their history and identity and as an opportunity to profile the host nation, far and beyond what was possible to achieve within the sporting arenas and the highly regulated Olympic ceremonies and protocol. The Mexico City 1968 Games provided one of the most ambitious arts festivals in Olympic history, spanning one year and acting as a showcase, not only for the best international art at the time, but also for the best of Mexican contemporary culture, as well as folklore and heritage. The ambition and quality of the programme demonstrated Mexico's advanced cultural and artistic expertise, which was in stark contrast to its status as a developing world nation in economic terms. In part, this achievement was possible because Mexico City viewed its cultural programme in a more holistic fashion than other Games hosts and, beyond the arts, incorporated discussions about education and science as well as advertising, design and communications. Montreal 1976 also presented an innovative cultural programme, emphasizing the connections between art and sport and exploring the presentation of arts activity within sporting venues, in particular the main Olympic Park avenue and the areas surrounding the stadium.

Throughout the 1960s and 1970s, other areas where artists and related creative practitioners made major contributions were through the design of banners and logos – what is now termed 'the look of the Games'. The imagery for Mexico City 1968, Tokyo 1964 and Munich 1972 are all exemplars of avant-garde visual design rather than simple marketing and branding exercises, which can be viewed as a foremost example of powerful cultural policy innovation emerging out of the Games. However, these elements of the Games were often not treated as part of the official cultural programme (Mexico City 1968 was a notable exception) and subsequent editions of the Games failed to use these environments as an expression of advanced place-sensitive creative practice.

The next stage in Olympic cultural programming was initiated with the Barcelona 1992 Olympic Bid, which proposed that the implementation of a Cultural Olympiad (a term already used in Mexico City 1968 amongst others) should in fact take place during the entire four years of the Olympiad – from the end of one Games edition to the start of the next. Thus, Barcelona's Cultural Olympiad started in 1988, at the end of the Seoul Games, and evolved up to 1992 with a different thematic emphasis for each year. Although it is not an IOC requirement, the four-year format has been maintained by subsequent Summer Games editions, while the Winter Games have also grown their ambitions for the Cultural Olympiad and presented the first full four-year Olympiad programme in the lead-up to Vancouver 2010.

This last stage in Olympic cultural programme development has been characterized by two main phenomena. On the one hand, there has been a clearer alignment of the programme with local and national cultural policy ambitions than ever before, where objectives have been set alongside national cultural event objectives. For example, this encompasses using the Games period not only to expand sport audiences but also cultural and arts audiences, and using the event to advance local creative development aspirations. It also includes development around social agendas, whereby the Olympics aspire to improve community inclusion, expanding access to marginal or deprived communities. Equally, Olympic cultural programmes today aim to strengthen local or national identity and are even intimately connected to wider economic agendas, such as repositioning cities through growing cultural tourism (García 2004). The kinds of political agendas that were common in previous periods have also been maintained, particularly for countries aspiring to overcome negative stereotypes related to their military past or human rights record, or for countries aspiring to present a more complex picture of their local identity, beyond fixed monocultural nation-state perceptions. Alternatively, the branding tension in relation to the main Olympic programme of sporting activity has become increasingly apparent, and there have been various attempts to establish separate Cultural Olympiads or Olympic Arts Festivals brands, with various degrees of success (García 2001).

However, a constant in the staging of Cultural Olympiads has been the lack of media attention and the extremely limited public recognition that such programmes arise (García 2001, 2008, 2010). While local authorities tend to see great value in highlighting the potential of a distinct cultural programme in their Olympic bid documents,[1] this is soon placed at a secondary level of importance once the Games are awarded and the demands surrounding the staging of the main sports programme become apparent. Protecting the cultural programme becomes less of a priority for organizing committees, given the lack of clearly defined guidelines from the IOC, which include nearly no oversight of accountability compared to other programmes. Also, the lack of protected sources of funding – including apparent clashes with Olympic sponsor priorities and media rights agreement – and the lack of regulation to ensure minimum levels of media coverage in the context of other Olympic activity places the cultural programme in a difficult position. This is not to say that strong artistic programmes are not developed, but that their synergy with other Olympic programmes has proved to be limited.

Some Olympic hosts, such as Barcelona 1992 and Athens 2004, viewed the Cultural Olympiad as a priority area, as the Games were expected to help advance a much wider cultural identity agenda for the city and nation. In these cases, the approach has been to establish the Cultural Olympiad as a separate company, with links to the Olympic Organizing Committee, but not fully integrated within it. Such an approach has allowed some independence of decision-making, but has also resulted in a noticeable disconnection between the cultural programme and other Olympic Games programmes. This has meant that the Olympic cultural programme has often been perceived as being completely separate from the Games. Such organizational division has not helped the cultural programme to overcome the ongoing funding, branding and media attention challenges it faces.

Sydney 2000 experimented with the notion of a distinct Olympic arts brand by making the most of the established structure for delivery within the Sydney Organizing Committee for the Olympic Games (SOCOG). The Olympic Arts Festivals team was located within SOCOG's marketing and special events division and the general manager for the cultural programme was also general manager for the Look of the Games programme. This meant that certain synergies were found in the approach to city dressing, and banners were displayed to showcase Olympic arts activity as well as Olympic sports activity. However, during the sixteen days of competition, the Olympic arts banners were removed, which meant that the notion of an Olympic arts brand was virtually non-existent at the time of greatest media attention on the city. The Winter Games in Torino 2006 also tried to establish a visible identity for their cultural offering by establishing a 'Look of the City' programme in parallel to their 'Look of the Games' programme. This meant that, while in the areas surrounding the sport venues, generic Look of the Games banners would prevail, in the city centre, particularly the grand 'piazzas', banners were all red exclusively (representing the notion of 'passion', which was the motto for the Games) and pictorial representations were all about iconic cultural attractions in the city (see García and Miah 2006). Vancouver 2010 also made some important advancements in maximizing visibility for their Olympic cultural programme brand by retaining distinct Cultural Olympiad banners throughout the city during the sixteen days of competition as well as the final lead-up year to the Games.

For London 2012, further branding innovation emerged, this time in establishing a Cultural Olympiad brand that did not conflict with the Olympic sponsor privilege. This was the primary achievement of the 'Inspired by London 2012' emblem, which we discussed in Chapter 2. The difference between the London 2012 Cultural Olympiad and the Inspired by London 2012 brands reveals a broader point about the different forms of cultural value associated with the Games. On the one hand, the local or national festival dimensions are articulated using the Inspired mark and are oriented towards those who will experience activities as live spectators in the lead-up to the Games. In contrast, there is the global media event, conveyed by the use of the Olympic symbol, which is mainly oriented towards broadcast audiences. With this separation, it becomes apparent that the Cultural Olympiad is clearly rooted within the local and national festival sphere, while only the cere-monies and sixteen days of sport programme are central to the Games as a global media spectacle.

OLYMPIC CULTURAL CAPITAL

The two World Wars were a defining period for the Olympic Games, as subsequently they quickly became a platform for show-casing national pride and identity (see Espy 1979). With the advent of television and live worldwide media coverage in the 1960s, they also progressively became a catalyst for the global branding of cul-tural identity, otherwise known as place marketing (Essex and Chalkley 1998). While some Games managed to fuse the sports with cultural aspirations – such as the diving venue at the Barcelona 1992 Games, with its impressive backdrop of the city – the sports programme generally did very little to facilitate this aspiration to transform or reinforce international impressions of cities and coun-tries. Even the transformation of an Olympic host city landscape has become an increasingly standardized phenomenon, with the same kinds of flags, banners and building wraps, leading to the para-doxical circumstance where cities as different as Sydney, Athens and Beijing are dressed following almost identical formats, with only slight design variations (García 2010).

This is why the cultural programme of an Olympic Games has had such value for host cities over the years, as it can be its distinguishing feature and the most effective platform to convey the identity and values of a nation. However, its direct value specifically to the local host, rather than the Olympic movement at large, also explains why the cultural programme has received only a limited prominence globally within the IOC's work. After all, it would make little sense for the IOC to impose expectations on the delivery of cultural activity that was not sensitive to local expertise or cultural priorities. Equally, the IOC's liaison with an OCOG is focused on the Games-time delivery, whereas an OCOG's cultural programme often exists in the years prior to the Games. Nevertheless, the consequence of this lack of involvement from the IOC has been that Olympic cultural programmes, while significant within their local context, have often failed to gain visibility within international Olympic circles or have failed to be perceived as a central dimension of the Olympic experience. An additional challenge in the representation of cultural values in the context of the Olympics has been the need to overcome the divide between meaningful local and national representation, and their translation into a global mediated arena (see Berkaak 1999; García 2001; MacAloon 1996; Moragas 1988, 1992).

In closing, Moragas (1992) and García (2008) note that the main sources for Olympic cultural capital are wide ranging and include the international and historical 'symbols' of the Olympic movement (such as the five rings, Olympic motto, etc.); the promotional strategy for specific Games editions and brand image of the host city (including 'Look of the Games' strategies); the Olympic ceremonies and rituals (including the torch relay); and the cultural activities programme or Cultural Olympiad.

All these elements can contribute to the creation of a determined image for the Games as well as the host-city culture. Furthermore, they are a powerful source for the transmission of values and identity signs that can assist in promoting the host city's cultural policy choices among the international media. For example, the choice of mascot design, Olympic emblem and the look of the Games in Barcelona 1992 was aimed at reflecting the contemporary, stylised and design-loving character of the city.

(García 2008: 365)

As such, the key to ensuring a memorable and valued cultural programme is to ensure a synergy between these overarching Olympic symbols and landmarks in the OCOG's delivery, and a sensitivity to the cultural strengths that operate within a host nation. One of the primary ways in which this is explored and advanced is through the Olympic ceremonies.

OPENING AND CLOSING CEREMONIES

Watched by an estimated audience of over 1 billion people world-wide, much has been written about the function of the opening and closing ceremonies as a platform for symbolic re-enactments of national identity, as well as a platform to showcase Olympic values (see MacAloon 1984; Moragas et al. 1996; Tomlinson 1996). The ceremonies have also often been a showcase for the latest innovation, as was demonstrated in Los Angeles 1984, when a jet pack was flown around the stadium by a 'rocket man', or at the Torino 2006 Games, which featured a Ferrari spinning around on ice. Alternatively, at the Beijing 2008 Olympic Games the precise choreography of 2,008 dancers within the opening ceremony and its sheer enormity of innovation became symbolic of China's emergence as a superpower and advanced, modern society (Jinxia 2010).

The ceremonies are also the primary mechanism through which the heritage of the Olympic movement is articulated to Olympic audiences through *constructed rituals*, strictly directed by IOC protocol as we discussed in Chapter 1. In contrast, the artistic element or cultural showcase section of an opening ceremony is overseen by the OCOG and has led to a variation of formats over the years. MacAloon identifies three main presentation models. These comprise the spectacular-show oriented 'impresario model' (e.g. Los Angeles 1984), the anthropologically oriented 'cultural experts model' with its focus on national folklore and cultural identity representation (e.g. Seoul 1988), and the 'auteur model' (e.g. Albertville 1992), char-acterized by an avant-garde artistic director (MacAloon 1984, 1996). In the case of the 'cultural experts model', it is the ritual that prevails, rather than entertainment, where the focus is on gestures and events that 'participants and congregants always know or think they know, in advance' (1996: 31). In contrast, when the 'impre-sario model' prevails, the focus is on spectacle and the 'unexpected'.

Finally, for the 'auteur model', the emphasis of the ceremony is on the artistic merit and 'unity of vision' (ibid. 37).

While there is no doubt that such moments can have a dramatic impact because of the viewing figures, or that they are an important opportunity to present a strong message about the host city and nation, they are also high-risk cultural artefacts for a host city as they can often present a reductive impression of the nation's identity, which locals may reject. Thus, as MacAloon notes, what is presented in an Olympic ceremony needs to reach a universal audience in a simultaneous framework and needs to be easily transmitted and interpreted through the media. As such, the event must be 'internationally sensitive to very different cultures' and 'avoid offending highly diverse and highly politicised social and cultural groups' (MacAloon 1996: 39-40). This tends to result in the 'regular production of historically deracinated, abstract and culturally neutered representations...of Olympic rituals' which may lead to simplistic interpretations by the public. Indeed, even the complexity of rather simple messages about a host nation's culture can be interpreted very differently across the 205 countries that are watching (Moragas et al. 1995), even though broadcasters are provided with a detailed script to accompany their commentary.[2]

OLYMPIC CULTURE THAT CHANGED THE WORLD

As we noted earlier, one of the key examples where the Olympic cultural dimensions fused with their broader symbols is in Leni Riefenstahl's film *Olympia*, produced in association with the so-called 'Nazi Olympics' of Berlin 1936 (Kruger 1998, Kruger and Murray 2003, Mandell 1971, Pitsula 2004). *Olympia* is a rare example of an Olympic cultural artefact that has transformed creative practice and shaped cultural debates beyond the Games context and the host nation, in this case, by exploring new approaches to film-making (Gunston 1960). Thus, *Olympia* is important not just for Olympic historians (Masumoto 1994), or for its symbolizing the problematic relationship between artists and politics. Rather, it is also important for film historians, as a ground-breaking contribution to the medium (Masumoto 1994, Schneider and Stier 2001). Its depiction of the athletic body and the Olympic symbols showcased new techniques in film-making while epitomizing the most important dimensions of the modern Olympic movement. Indeed, the Olympic Games have often lent themselves to storytelling through film-making, where other important historical artefacts include such titles as *Chariots of Fire* (Hudson 1981) *One Day in September* (Macdonald 1999), *Munich* (Spielberg 2006) and, most recently, *With Glowing Hearts* (Lavaigne 2010), a film about the Vancouver 2010 Olympic social media community.

Television has also made an important contribution to the cultural history of the Olympics, although it often achieves only local importance for the host nation. For example, on the approach to London 2012, the BBC commissioned a television comedy series – a mockumentary – called *Twenty Twelve* (Morton 2011). This series tracked the work of a fictional OCOG – the Olympic Deliverance Commission – as it bumbled its way through organizing the Olympic Games. Storylines focused on aspects of the Games that had been widely scrutinized by the media, such as glitches in transportation, protecting the brand and the ambiguity of the Cultural Olympiad. Indeed, some reporting of the programme claimed that what was being satirized in the programme was actually happening in the real organizing committee, for instance, a story about technical problems with the Olympic Games countdown clock (Gibson 2011). In itself, the series provides an insight into British culture and is worthy of discussing in terms of what it conveys about the identity of Britain. However, even more interesting is how *Twenty Twelve* is situated alongside another similar mockumentary produced ten years earlier around the Sydney 2000 Olympic Games, titled *The Games*. In the case of the latter, beyond exposing similar operational issues and media controversies, this series was able to capture Australia's imagination with regard to Aboriginal reconciliation, an issue that attracted considerable debate but was never properly addressed via the formal structures of government during Games time. There was no apology from the government about the country's history of systematic neglect of Aboriginal interests at that point in time. However, the series staged a fictional apology that was eloquent, moving and a sincere characterization of the sentiment felt by those who had argued on behalf of Aboriginal reconciliation for years (Permezel 2000). In this regard, the coexistence of such series with the Games hosting process neatly illustrates how the Games become a vehicle for not just expressions of cultural production excellence, but also for negotiations of national cultural aspirations and identity. In this sense, cultural artefacts such as satirical television shows may placate the masses, who otherwise may feel considerable disaffection or anger at the Games hosting process.

These examples demonstrate two important ways in which the Olympic Games' cultural dimensions define what is historically important about an Olympic Games. First, they reveal how the Games can be an opportunity to address entrenched issues about social identity, by providing a platform and pressure for key stakeholders to work together over a period of time and address differences. Second, it reveals how often the more interesting aspects of Olympic cultural practice do not emerge from the Organizing Committees or official Cultural Olympiads. This is not to say that the key actors involved with their production are completely outside the Olympic family. Yet, each of them enjoys a varied relationship with Olympic officialdom. Riefenstahl's *Olympia* was a film commissioned by the Berlin Games' organizers and became the official 1936 Olympic film, but it was not treated as part of the official Olympic programme or 'Olympic art competitions'. In contrast, the producers of *The Games* and *Twenty Twelve* were also official media partners to the Games – ABC for Sydney 2000 and BBC for London 2012. As such, their products cannot be seen as entirely detached from the Olympic family. Yet, they are examples of the cultural legacies that begin to develop at the moment when an Olympic Games is awarded, which become a catalyst for a range of cultural and artistic reactions, regardless of whether they are formally packaged as Olympic cultural programme activities. As noted earlier, other examples of important creative innovation at the Games include the advancement of graphic design practices, as showcased during Mexico City 1968, Munich 1972 or Barcelona 1992, which inspired designers for generations to come (see Schiller and Young 2010).

EDUCATION REFORM THROUGH OLYMPISM

Given Coubertin's focus on the 'Youth of the World' as the primary vehicle for and target of the Olympic movement, coupled with his career as an educator, it may come as no surprise to point out that each Olympic Games comes with an extensive Olympic education programme. One of the primary overlapping artefacts between culture and education is the IOC Olympic Museum in Lausanne, an entity that Coubertin aspired to create. Yet, the Olympic commitment to education goes even deeper than this. As we noted in Chapter 1, the primary vehicles for Olympic education are the International Olympic Academy in Greece and the National Olympic Academies, which sit within the National Olympic Committees. Moreover, Olympic scholarship and research has existed for many decades and is an integral part of the critical intellectual community that surrounds the Olympic movement. However, the concept of Olympic education has been marginalized within education and research. One is unlikely to find Coubertin's *Olympism* taught within an undergraduate philosophy degree, or within any other subject than physical education within a secondary school syllabus. These circumstances speak to how the Olympics have become renowned for their sports events over and above any other dimension and how their development has been driven by the media spectacle and fan-based culture of elite sports.

FESTIVAL VERSUS SPECTACLE

While 99.9 per cent of the Olympic audience experience the Games through some form of media, one may still argue that the Olympic Games are meant to be experienced live. This claim does not simply appeal to the idea that sports performances are best experienced without any mediating device. Indeed, with increasing technological capabilities, this elevation of the live experience may eventually be contested. Rather, it is to acknowledge that the day-to-day Olympic experience extends far beyond what takes place within the competition venues, transforming the city into a mega-festival, rather than just a mega-event. In this respect, experiencing the Olympic Games live can often be a transformative moment, with many Olympic fans committing their lives to returning to the Games because of its unique festival atmosphere. The main wealth of Olympic cultural value lies in the opportunities for lived inter-cultural exchange across participants as well as spectators and residents and the global platform it provides for a particular city and nation to make a cultural statement that is globally meaningful as well as owned by its community. Protecting Olympic cultural programming as integral to the implementation of the sixteen days of sports competition can ensure that the richness and complexity of host cultures come to the fore and provide a distinct identity to each edition of the Games, beyond the limitations of standard global branding techniques. Furthermore, by making the most of local cultural production practices in the context of such an international mega-event, the Games can shape local cultural policy and contribute towards greater intercultural understanding and exchange.

This need to expand the Olympic Games experience beyond the sport competition realm is currently being advocated by the executive Games production teams within the IOC in what is now termed the '360 Games Management Philosophy' (IOC 2009a: 13). In the first instance, this is largely reliant on revisiting and expanding the interpretation and implementation of the Games' cultural dimensions. Such ambition started to become manifest in the guidelines for the 2016 Olympic Games candidate cities and is further specified for the 2018 candidate cities. In the lead-up to 2016, for the first time in a candidature questionnaire, references to the Games' cultural component are not relegated to a minor chapter with little relation to other bid sections, but placed at the heart of what is defined as the 'Olympic Experience', in parallel to sport, torch, ceremonies and other city activities. This could mean that, after over a century operating at the margins of Games delivery and media representation, the official Olympic cultural programme is becoming more integrated within other aspects of the Games and, as in the case of opening and closing ceremonies, has the opportunity to become a core source of iconic symbolic and cultural value.

The challenge and the opportunity for organizers and policy-makers is to ensure that the pressure to respond to global media needs does not diminish the complexity of localized, distinct and diverse cultural narratives. However, very little may be advanced by an OCOG's cultural mission or the IOC's cultural policy without first coming to terms with structural obstacles within the Olympic movement. For example, if one examines the range of bodies that are recognized by the IOC or its partners, there is no clear integration of the culture or education sectors that Coubertin expected to blend with sport, with the possible exception of the IOC's University Relations department, which is allied to its Olympic

Studies Centre. Yet, there are no International Cultural Federations that exist which could work with the IOC in a way that is equivalent to the International Sports Federations. Moreover, IOC members tend to have a sports background rather than cultural or education-driven careers. The problem with this lack of cultural sensitivity is made apparent in situations like the recent episode when Team GB athletics coach Charles van Commenee announced publicly that track and field athletes would be forbidden from participating in the London 2012 opening ceremony. His comments show complete insensitivity to the importance of the athlete's wider Olympic experience, beyond winning a medal (Kessel 2011). Indeed, he likened contributing to the ceremony to 'going shopping', which reveals how little regard the sports industries have for the wider aspects of Olympism – precisely the aspects of the Olympics that are supposed to make the event so special for athletes.

Thus, given the dominance of the narrow interest of the sports industries, the future of culture at the Olympics remains uncertain. Perhaps it should work towards something like the UN's Agenda 21 for Culture in the same way that the IOC worked towards Agenda 21 for the Environment (see Chapter 5). Indeed, within Chapter 8 we argue that when thinking about Olympic legacies and impacts, culture is central to all other Olympic legacies, a view that coheres with Hawkes's (2001) 'fourth pillar' of sustainable development.

These concerns may not be quite as problematic for education as they are for culture. After all, it is common for athletes either to come to sport from an educational background or to go on to be involved with Olympic education through coaching after retiring from competition. Furthermore, there are no comparable international networks of organizations dedicated to representing cultural practices or interests at IOC level as there are for sport. All the same, the positions of both culture and education in the Olympic experience remain fragile. Of course, there are significant additional challenges in programming culture and education as opposed to sport within an Olympic context, not least of which is that artists and educators often appeal to an intellectual freedom that may challenge the IOC's desire to control the Olympic communication messages. Moreover, the hyper-commercial world of the Olympics may not suit cultural or education programming, even though many of the largest cultural events in the world today also rely on commercial sponsorship and despite the fact that, in the education world, there are such places as the Hamburger University of McDonalds. Yet, without a cultural and education programme that is sensitive to local interests and global audiences, the Games are reduced to mere spectacle, focused solely on breaking world records and throwing a good party rather than addressing its broader humanitarian aspirations.

POLITICS AND DIPLOMACY

In May 2011, the IOC's 9th World Conference on Sport and Environment took place in Doha in partnership with the United Nations Environmental Programme (UNEP). In a closing session of the conference, a journalist asked the IOC President Jacques Rogge to comment on the killing of Osama Bin Laden. In response, President Rogge said: 'What happened to Mr. Bin Laden is a political issue on which I do not wish to comment' (Hersh 2011). This incident reignited a debate within the international media about the way in which the Olympic movement negotiates political issues and two interesting questions emerge from it that require our consideration when attempting to make sense of the relationship between politics and the Olympics. First, why would the IOC President respond in such a dispassionate way, given the widespread condemnation of international terrorism, which Osama Bin Laden has come to symbolize for many nations? Second, we must ask why a journalist would expect the IOC President to answer such a question in the first place and this speaks to the public expectations that operate around the Olympic movement.

These two questions provide an entry point for a debate about the relationship between politics and the Olympics. By answering them, we will learn how their relationship is terribly complicated, sometimes contradictory, but always consequential. As such, this chapter discusses the complex political histories of the Olympic movement, which demonstrate how its work is often inextricable from wider political ambitions. In so doing, we consider the different political actors within the Olympic community, who may seek to utilize the Olympics to promote Olympic or non-Olympic political campaigns (athletes, IOC, NOCs, governments). Furthermore, we consider what this means for how we make sense of the IOC, the Olympic Games and the movement. We also explore some of the consequences of the IOC's political relationships and activities over the years, particularly its link with the UN and examples of when the Games have been a vehicle for what may be called quiet diplomacy or public diplomacy. Throughout these discussions, we reveal some of the ways in which the Olympic Games have provoked political campaigns and protests, the consequences of which have been a drive to achieve greater control over the public within the Olympic city, via anti-terrorism measures or crowd management. Finally, we return to these two initial questions about Bin Laden and the IOC President Jacques Rogge, whereupon we should be clearer about the explanation for his answer and the merit of the IOC's position of maintaining neutrality on such matters.

To understand more about Jacques Rogge's response to the journalist, it is necessary to offer some context by discussing how the Olympics have been politicized in the past and how this affects the present orientation towards political matters which is, we suggest, deliberately cautious. The Olympic movement's orientation towards political issues is difficult to discern. Historically, the IOC has persistently advocated the idea that the Olympic movement should not engage with political issues or national governmental matters and, instead, confine itself to the business of sport. This view is born out of the IOC's primary desire to ensure that as many countries from around the world as possible feel able to align themselves with the Olympic values and send their athletes to the Games. Indeed, the scale of this challenge should not be understated. After all, while the UN presently has 192 member states, there are 205 within the Olympic family. As such, ensuring that each of these countries is able to put politics aside in order to compete in sport is a remarkable diplomatic achievement. Indeed, this relatively uncomplicated aspiration has not always been successful, with countries choosing not to participate at various Games for reasons of political disagreement, as we will go on to discuss. So great is this concern that the Olympic Charter requires Olympic family members to undertake 'No kind of demonstration or political, religious or racial propaganda … in any Olympic sites, venues or other areas' (IOC 2010a: 98) during the Games. The scope of these rules includes the wearing of clothing with symbols or messages of a political nature and any violation may lead to exclusion from the Games, as determined by the IOC Executive Board.

ACTIVISM AND PROTEST

Despite these guidelines, some of the most memorable moments in modern Olympic history have been made possible by individuals who ignored the IOC rules, or who have utilized their Olympic affiliation to make some important political point. Indeed, at most Olympic Games, there have been some forms of political activism, either from accredited persons, such as athletes, or from organizations which have built campaigns around the Games period (Adi and Miah 2011, Lenskyj 2002). For example, in 1968, the US athletes Tommie Smith and John Carlos used their place on the winners' podium to give their 'black power' salute in support of African American civil rights (Hartman 1996). They were accompanied by the third man on the podium, Peter Norman, an Australian athlete who won the Silver medal and who was wearing a badge for the 'Olympic Project for Human Rights' on his left breast. Smith and Carlos were suspended from the US team the following day by IOC President and fellow American Avery Brundage, but the legacy of their actions lives on.

Such moments become historically important for the Olympic Games and society more widely, even though they compromise the neutral space of the Olympic programme. They represent the contradictions of the Olympic movement, whereby the Charter espouses universal values, but where it is compelled to sanction advocates of similar values, which may not yet be recognized as worthy of universal support, in this case the fight against racial prejudice. Yet, it is not only athletes who are able to enact moments of Olympic activism. In recent times, celebrities have also played an important role in articulating objections to controversial Olympic issues. For example, on the approach to Beijing 2008, US actress Mia Farrow and her son Ronan Farrow campaigned against what she called China's 'Genocide Olympics', drawing attention to its support of the Sudanese government, which was involved with sponsoring mass killings in the Darfur region of Sudan (Farrow and Farrow 2007).

Of course, individual activism occurs mostly from those who are not well known, through membership of political groups or communities. At the Vancouver 2010 Games, protests took place over the neglect of housing rights for disadvantaged populations, most visibly articulated by the 'Olympic Tent Village', where the city's homeless people located themselves during the Games. Sometimes, protests can emerge from communities that have established political concerns, which then become engaged by the Olympics. Alternatively, the Olympics may create new communities which are unified by their common frustrations over the Games. This is true of the 'No Sochi 2014 Committee' campaign, which has criticized the location of the Olympic facilities on what it describes as the site of the 'Circassian Genocide', a historical site which they feel should be protected as a sign of respect to those who died.[1]

The scale of such coordinated action can be vast. For example, on the approach to the Beijing 2008 Games, the range of these actions was apparent through the work of Amnesty International, Human Rights Watch, Reporters Without Borders, and Team Darfur, each of which campaigned around some aspect of China's governmental actions or policies. Their interventions included unofficial, leaked Amnesty International poster campaigns, which went viral online, depicting violent scenes within a sporting context (Hutcheon 2008) However, perhaps most dramatic of all were interventions associated with the Beijing 2008 Olympic programme itself. First of all, there was an intervention at the torch-lighting ceremony in ancient Olympia by Jean-François Julliard, a member of the press freedom organization Reporters Without Borders. While the Beijing 2008 President Lio Qi was giving a speech, Julliard managed to enter the television cameras' view and stand directly behind Qi, whereupon he unfurled a protest banner depicting the Olympic rings as handcuffs with the word 'Beijing 2008'. While this managed to disrupt the proceedings, the Greek cameras quickly switched their feed away from the speaker's podium and

Chinese television cut away, leaving most people unaware that anything had happened. On the same day, pro-Tibet protesters were in the village of ancient Olympia, burning flags and attempting to interrupt the torch relay. Second, there were widespread manifestations that took place around the international leg of the torch relay from Paris to San Francisco. Most dramatic of all was the moment when a protester interrupted the progress of the torch while it was in London. The torch bearer Konnie Huq was tackled to the floor by a protester, who was quickly taken away by the Chinese police who were guarding the flame. So dramatic were these pro-Tibet protests that the IOC subsequently decreed that 2008 would be the last time an international leg of the relay would take place, limiting future relays to the symbolic lighting in Greece followed by a route within the host nation only.

TERRORISM AND SECURITY

While often symbolically meaningful, these examples of political manifestation generally have only a limited impact on the smooth running of the Olympics. However, when campaigns are driven by organizations which are able to invest resources strategically into seriously disrupting the Olympics, the consequences can be considerably more severe. Indeed, it is these moments that are more directly influential in the IOC's hard line against politicizing the Olympics. The most consequential of such actions are those that are characterized as terrorism. Indeed, speaking at the IOC Congress in 2002, President Jacques Rogge stated that 'The events in Munich, those of 11 September and the re-emergence of international terrorism make security the number one priority for any sports organisation' (Rogge 2002a).

As part of the risk assessment for a candidate city, terrorist threat and the capabilities of the local forces (civilian and military) are thus an important part of the evaluation process. The most infamous act of terrorism at the Olympic Games occurred at the Munich 1972 Games, when a Palestinian group disguised as athletes traversed the six-foot-high fence of the Olympic athletes' village and entered the Israeli compound, taking nine members of the team hostage and killing two. While the German authorities attempted to resolve the situation without any further bloodshed, it was not to be and all of the hostages eventually lost their lives, in what was widely described as a bungled attempt to rescue them while negotiating with the terrorists (Toohey and Taylor 2008). However, Munich is not the only example of terrorism at the Games. Another notable example was Atlanta 1996 when Eric Robert Rudolph planted a pipe bomb in the Olympic recreational area called Olympic Centennial Park. The bomb exploded, killing two people and injuring over 100 more. While Rudolph did express that he had problems with the Olympic 'socialist' ideology, his testimony indicated that his primary motivation was to embarrass the Clinton administration (Rudolph 2005). Significantly, however, this episode was not the only bomb threat that was received at the Atlanta 1996 Olympic Games (Toohey and Veal 2007). Indeed, terror threats have been a common feature of many other Olympics, such as concerns about North Korea taking military action over the Seoul 1988 Games, or the regional terrorist group ETA taking action against the Barcelona 1992 Games, to name just two other high-risk situations. As a result, concerns about terrorism have traditionally been a dominant feature of political priorities around the Olympic Games (Richards et al. 2011).

The impact of these events on the organization of mega-events generally, but the Olympics specifically, has been dramatic, with security occupying a significant part of the host city's budget and driving a number of priorities in terms of how the Games are staged. Indeed, from ticketing to volunteer recruitment, there is barely an area of the Olympic programme that is unaffected by security procedures. This situation has been heightened considerably after the 9/11 attacks on the USA and Kellner notes how, 'as the Winter Olympics opened in Salt Lake City on February 8, it featured more troops and police than were stationed in Afghanistan' (Kellner 2003: 25). As a result, the experience of being at an Olympic Games today is quite different from any pre-2002 edition, as there is now a significantly visible presence of armed guards and high-security measures at all Olympic venues and there are large areas of the city cordoned off for the exclusive use and protection of Olympic family members. Of course, the appeal of the Olympics to terrorist groups stems from the fact that they are a mega-event with great media appeal and thus an enormous reach into people's homes. Indeed, as noted by the Black September spokesperson a week following the Munich 1972 attacks,

> The Olympiad arouses the people's interest and attention more than anything else in the world. The choice of the Olympics, from the purely propagandistic viewpoint was 100 per cent successful. It was like painting the name of Palestine on a mountain that can be seen from the four corners of the earth.
>
> (Dershowitz, cited in Toohey and Taylor 2008: 459-60)

Given the prominence of the Games, it is important not to understate the burden of making them secure. However, it is equally important not to conclude that the pursuit of their security legitimates a complete disregard for individual freedoms around the Olympic city, either before or during the Games. Yet, this is often what takes place. For example, while the Beijing 2008 Games took place with relatively few incidents, this was widely seen to be as a result of heavy-handed tactics to control dissident voices in the lead-up to the Games and such approaches may be seen as having compromised other social values (McRoskey 2010). Clearly, the organization of any mega-event involves some restrictions on the freedom of visitors or local citizens, either in how traffic is managed, or in how public spaces are organized. However, this should not extend into other areas, such as putting greater restrictions on freedom of speech during the Games period. Indeed, ever sensitive to these potential criticisms, the BOCOG indicated that protest zones had been organized for activists to use during the Games, a practice not common in China. Yet, there is very little evidence that they were used to any great effect.

Some researchers have noted that the prospect of hosting an Olympic Games may be used by city or national leaders to increase their security measures aggressively, on the grounds that this is necessary to secure the Games (Fussey 2011). Indeed, the fact that these heightened measures are rarely lowered following the successful completion of the Games supports this view (Rodriguez 2011). Moreover, such is the hype around securing the Games that the Olympics may contribute 'to a climate of fear, heightened security and surveillance' (Surveillance Studies Centre 2009). Rodriguez (2011) refers to a Wikileaks document, which makes explicit how the Olympics are an opportunity for governments to assert their national interest by working with other governments to build robust security systems. An important dimension of this is the business opportunities it creates and the political leverage it may bring. Indeed, a number of cross-national networks exist to support host cities in their efforts to secure the Games, including the Olympic Security Advisory Group and the Olympic Intelligence Centre.

The Olympics are also a multinational security concern, not least because all competing nations have their own citizens present at the event. This leads unavoidably to a situation in which all nations have a stake in the security performance of the host nation and often invest considerably in assisting the implementation of security plans. In another Wikileaks document, a report for the US Congress by Halchin (2004) outlines how the FBI, CIA, Department of Defense and Department of State were all engaged with plans to make the Athens 2004 Olympics secure, itself a consequence of how 9/11 changed the US administration (United States Government Accountability Office 2005). Moreover, in some cases, the attendance of a particular nation may be seen as a threat by another attending nation or the host nation itself. For example, during the Cold War in the lead-up to the Los Angeles 1984 Games, the US Government was acutely aware of the challenge posed by the USSR's attendance, as this White House directive articulates:

> In hosting the Games in this manner, it is the United States policy to ensure the establishment of all possible measures to prevent intelligence losses and reduce the vulnerability of national security actvities to the hostile intelligence threat resulting from the Soviet flights or ship visit.
>
> (The White House 1984: 1)

Finally, given the prominence of security concerns, one may even argue that the Olympics can be thought of as a weapons-trading fairground, as cutting-edge technology is brought in by the host nation to increase its ability to manage what is often the largest single police operation of any country.

GOVERNMENT AGENDAS AND BOYCOTTS

While counter-terrorism and security strategies are now established mechanisms of a government's role in staging an Olympic Games, political interests around the Olympic Games are also at times defined by acts of government. Indeed, Dayan and Katz (1992: 201) note that events such as the Olympics are mechanisms that 'reinforce the status of leaders' and, as such, attract political posturing from leaders, for example, by being seen with the Olympic torch. The close proximity of government ministers to Olympic affairs is a further indication of how the Olympics may be seen to be in the service of political development. Furthermore, in many of the countries where there exists an NOC, there is also often legislation in place to protect the Olympic brand. For example, in the United Kingdom, Olympic legislation has been in place since 1995 with the Olympic Symbol Etc (Protection) Act 1995, which was amended in 2006 after securing the rights to host the London 2012 Games (*London Olympic and Paralympic Games Act 2006*). Also, there are some areas of Olympic interests that cross over with other political priorities, such as legislation around doping offences. In this case, there exists an increasing pressure from the IOC and the World Anti-Doping Agency for countries to introduce criminal actions, rather than just civil prosecutions against doping. Among the various mechanisms for coordinating an Olympic Games, it is also commonplace to appoint a dedicated Olympics minister who oversees the work of the public sector involved with delivering the Games, thus making an explicit link between the event and national government agendas.

However, it is what the IOC considers to be illegitimate acts towards the Olympic movement that tend to present the largest government-initiated challenges for an OCOG and IOC, namely boycotts or nationally sanctioned non-participation at the Games. These moments are good examples of how nuanced is the position of the Olympics with regard to political discourse and action. After all, in cases of national non-participation, it is difficult to hold the IOC accountable for this occurrence, unless one believes that its decision to have awarded the Games to a country that has specific, ongoing conflicts is itself politically naïve. Of course, the complexity of world politics is such that, at the time of awarding the Games, the disputes may be vastly different in magnitude compared to when the Games actually take place. As such, one can understand that basing decisions about which country is entitled to host the Games on political disagreements or conflicts would leave the Olympics very vulnerable, especially as there is not always an abundance of nations prepared to host the Games.

Over the last century, there have been many examples of non-participation at an Olympics, including Melbourne 1956 (not attended by Egypt, Iraq, Lebanon, the Netherlands, People's Republic of China, Spain, Switzerland), Tokyo 1964 (Indonesia, North Korea), Montreal 1976 (Tanzania and twenty-two African Nations), Seoul 1988 (North Korea, Albania, Cuba, Ethiopia, Madagascar, Nicaragua, Seychelles). However, it is perhaps the Cold War period that is most remembered for the extensive boycotts against the Moscow 1980 and Los Angeles 1984 Games, which included various allies of each nation teaming up against the other: around sixty countries allied with the USA against participation at the Moscow Games and fourteen with Russia against participation at Los Angeles (Kanin 1980). Yet, boycotts are not only enacted by governments. At the Melbourne 1956 Games, the initial signs of boycotts came from the world's media, which refused to cover the Games, after being expected 'to pay royalties for the privilege of showing Olympic newsfilm on a delayed basis' (Wenn 1993). Importantly, in moments of non-participation or conflict situations, the IOC still has scope to permit the participation of athletes who, instead of competing under their nation's flag, can compete under the Olympic flag, thus effectively overstepping their country's political decision.

THE IOC AS A POLITICAL BODY

Despite the many examples of the Olympic movement having been subject to the political will of others, it would be wrong to suggest that these processes are all unidirectional acts imposed upon the Olympic movement. In actual fact, the IOC has often engaged in acts that may be seen as inherently political, though it is in these examples that differences of opinion arise over what kind of function they serve. Returning to Coubertin's vision of Olympism, one may argue that the Olympics must be seen as an inherently political project, which has an ideology at its heart and, through its pursuit of inter-governmental cooperation, is unavoidably operating as a political entity. Of course, this is not a view that Coubertin espoused explicitly. Thus, awarding a city the right to host the Olympic Games may be construed as a political act in itself and some commentators from both within the IOC and outside it have argued that the decision of its members to award the Games to a particular place may sometimes be influenced by the desire to bring about some form of positive social change. Indeed, IOC President Jacques Rogge (2008) alludes to this when noting that 'the Olympic Movement, and the Paralympic Movement, has often been the catalyst for social, urban and political change'.

Sometimes, the decision to award a Games to a particular place may have required the IOC to immerse itself deep within global political relations, as was true of Seoul 1988 (Manheim 1990, Pound 1994). Yet, at other times, this can lead to a host nation's exploitation of the Olympic Games, as was true of the Berlin 1936 Games, which took place under Hitler's administration. These Games were the first time that expressions of national identity were tied to the Games' visual aesthetic. Moreover, Berlin was the Games that created the Olympic torch relay, which is widely thought to have been a mechanism of Nazi propaganda, as noted in Chapter 3. The decision to host a Games in a politically controversial location may also expose or exacerbate conflicts between nations. For example, the decision to host the 2008 Games in Beijing became one of the most controversial choices the IOC has ever made. Indeed, Mastrocola (1995: 142) notes that in a previous bidding process where Beijing was a favourite candidate against Sydney, the eventual winner, the US Government 'officially expressed its opposition to Beijing hosting the 2000 Olympics in congressional resolutions'. The basis for their opposition was China's human rights record which, in their view, was not 'consistent with the Olympic ideal'. To give another example, for some time in the lead-up to the 2008 Games, China's relations with Taiwan were strained over whether the torch would go through the country or not. Strong Taiwanese resistance meant that this did not happen after all. Also, given the controversies around Tibet and Darfur at the time, Beijing 2008 became the subject of demands to boycott the Games within the international media. Although full national boycotts did not materialize, some heads of state, such as Angela Merkel from Germany, decided to decline the invitation to attend the opening ceremony and this was seen by many as a political gesture.

Alternatively, decisions about where the Games are awarded can result in political benefits that may accrue for a particular region of the world. Traditionally, there was a perception that IOC votes tended to favour Europe above other continents, which has been host to 50 per cent of all summer Games to date. This is in stark contrast with the situation in Africa, which has yet to host the Games, and Latin America, which hosted its first Games in Mexico in 1968, followed only by Rio de Janeiro in 2016, the first host city in South America some 120 years after the beginning of the modern Olympic Games. While these decisions are more likely to be governed by the merit of the bid than the politics of the place, before the IOC reforms in 2000 it was much more difficult to rule out political and financial bias in how IOC votes were cast (see Chapter 5). Indeed, despite the reforms, it remains likely that IOC members will still have personal geographical biases, in the same way that global politics also gives rise to regional factions. Whether this is seen as a corrupting element of the Games or an inherent bias to any global entity is open for debate, though it is important to stress how much the bidding process regulations have changed since the reforms.

In defence of the IOC's pursuit of apolitical status, one may evaluate its actions over the last century as a commitment towards pursuing strictly humanitarian causes, notably peace. There are various ways in which this can be evidenced, the most important of which is a relatively recent alliance between the UN and the IOC through the Olympic Truce (Briggs et al. 2004, Georgiadis and Strigas 2008). The Truce is a campaign which was revived in 1991, embodying the ancient Greek tradition of Ekecheiria (holding of hands), which was in place during the ancient Olympic Games and which involved seeking agreements across the Greek city states to encourage the cessation of conflicts in order to ensure safe passage of athletes to Olympia for the Games. It is now widely believed that this commitment, while ensuring athletes did make it to Olympia, did not have the effect of suspending conflict during the period. Nevertheless, this aspiration now occupies the attention of the IOC and the UN for the modern Games. Moreover, this is a project that clearly articulates the way in which the IOC sees its role in international politics as the Truce aims to protect, 'as far as possible, the interests of the athletes and sport in general, and to contribute to the search for peaceful and diplomatic solutions to the world's conflicts' (IOC 2009b). The IOC outlines its original Truce campaign as follows:

> The first Olympic Truce project was launched in 1991, following the break-up of the Federal Republic of Yugoslavia and the creation of the

United Nations (UN) Security Council Sanctions Committee against this country, as a result of which, in 1992, its Resolution 757 included 'sport' as a sanctioned element for the first time. ... On the advice of the Executive Board, on 21 July 1992 the 99th IOC Session launched a call to all States, as well as all international and national organisations, and asked the IOC President to start talks with the UN. Finally, the UN Security Council Sanctions Committee and the IOC reached an agreement enabling the Yugoslav athletes to take part as individuals in the Games of the XXV Olympiad in 1992 in Barcelona.

(IOC 2009b)

Every two years, just a few months before the opening of the Olympic Games, the IOC President attends the UN General Assembly calling on Heads of States to cease conflicts for the period of the Olympic Games. Today, Organizing Committees for the Games develop specific programmes of work to advance the ideals of the Olympic Truce. Moreover, a formal International Olympic Truce Foundation has been set up with a primary base in Lausanne and a symbolic home in Olympia, while an Olympic Truce Centre has also been established in Athens.

Such work is typical of how the IOC interprets its apolitical role as an organization involved with the promotion of peace through sports participation, very much along the lines of the so-called 1971 'Ping Pong' diplomacy, where China and the USA achieved cooperation through sport after a long period of difficult relations (Quoqi 2008). The extent of this Olympic contribution to diplomacy includes a number of symbolic achievements.[2] For instance, it provided an opportunity for North and South Korea to enter a single team at the Sydney 2000 Olympic Games. At the same Games, it also provided the emerging sovereign state of East Timor with a mechanism to send its athletes to the Games competing under an 'Independent Olympic Athletes' flag, which also symbolically announced their emergence to the world.

At the same time, the IOC is able to suspend a nation from the Olympic movement, if it is seen to have contravened the Olympic Charter. For instance, after the Second World War, Germany and Japan were not invited to the London 1948 Olympic Games. At Tokyo 1964, South Africa was also expelled from the Olympics, because of its support of apartheid, which violated the fundamental principles of the Olympic Charter. South Africa would be banned from the Olympic Games until the end of apartheid, being welcomed back for the first time at the Barcelona 1992 Games. At other times, a country may be suspended from the Games because of internal conflicts which make it unable to function as a nation, as was the case for Afghanistan, which was suspended in 1999 and could not attend the Sydney 2000 Games due to its being under Taliban rule, a system of belief that forbade women from participating in sport.

The IOC also has considerable political leverage, which allows it to make certain demands of countries which other organizations might not achieve. For instance, at the Beijing 2008 Games, when the media was having difficulty getting onto the Internet to report the Games while in China, the IOC intervened, declaring that China would be in breach of contract if it failed to open its media restrictions to foreign reporters. While this may be seen as an example of how the Olympics can change the politics of a nation, it is important to note that the IOC's request was limited exclusively to the reporting of sports during the Games hosting period. Nevertheless, it is perhaps one example of what Mastrocola (1995: 152) describes when saying that, 'although the nongovernmental bodies of the Olympic organization cannot alone compel government compliance, their rules, regulations, and decisions help determine state practice and best articulate a customary or autonomous sports law'.[3]

Despite this array of political interventions by the IOC, there is no uniform approach to how it deals with political matters. In some sense, the IOC is an organization that has responded to the conditions of its time, taking the lead on key issues as they become important for society to address. This may be said about the participation of women in sport and the desire to ensure non-discrimination generally across Olympic participation. While some IOC Presidents, such as Juan Antonio Samaranch, have made clear attempts to progress political issues by utilizing the movement's leverage with national leaders, others have clearly avoided such work, focusing instead on other matters, such as fighting doping or the pursuit of re-engaging the 'youth of the world', as may be said of the IOC's current President who instituted the Youth Olympic Games in 2010.

ARE THE OLYMPICS ABOVE POLITICS?

In part, what makes the relationship between the Olympics and politics so fascinating is the range of ways in which historically important political issues have been addressed through acts undertaken at the Games and the manner in which the IOC negotiates political matters. If one accepts that the role of self-defined social movements like the Olympics is to advance broad humanitarian causes, then rules that suppress such actions would seem counterproductive or even hypocritical. However, the challenge for the IOC is that many such causes – indeed any humanitarian concern – may always unavoidably be tied to some form of ideology, even if this ideology appeals to principles that many take to be values that ought to be universally shared, such as respect for human dignity and non-discrimination.

One of the challenges is that the Olympics are not a singular entity that can be neatly characterized as a particular kind of organization. Rather, they consist of a wide spectrum of organizations and relationships, each with particular international and domestic functions. For instance, until his death in 2003, the Iraq Olympic Committee was led by Uday Hussein, son of the country's then leader Saddam Hussein. To this end, the associations of many people linked with the Olympic movement are deeply political. Certainly, the IOC is often at the forefront of political matters, but even its role and scope of activity have changed dramatically over the last century. Thus, in a relatively short period of time, it has become a global power of non-governmental influence and guardian of one of the most lucrative global brands, with many of the world's largest transnational corporations vying for exclusive contracts.

In sum, we argue that the Olympics must be seen as a force for political and social change – positive and negative – and that this realization should shape its terms of business. As Black and Bezanson (2004) note, the decision to bid for an Olympic Games is often a politically informed decision. Indeed, these are views that have some resonance with how people within the IOC see their work. For instance, Mallon (2006) notes that former IOC President Juan Antonio Samaranch, was 'once quoted as saying that the mere act of declaring the group non-political is, itself, a political statement' (p. xcviii). Equally, many of the issues we identified in

Chapter 2 have political implications – such as advocating gender equality within society, which aligns the Olympic movement with particular belief systems. Even the recognition of some nations rather than others may be seen as a political act.

Yet, to return to our initial questions within this chapter, President Jacques Rogge's refusal to comment on the death of Bin Laden may be explained by examining the particular line that is taken in the context of the IOC's politically sensitive activities – which is to involve itself solely on matters related to sport. Importantly, Rogge was not asked about his views on the morality of terror, as an act of war, or whether he regarded the plight of the Taliban to be worthy of respect. If Rogge had been asked these questions, he might have been more inclined to argue that acts of terrorism are an affront to the Olympic Charter in their failure to respect other nations, as he might also have deplored acts of war that threaten the Olympic Games.[4] After all, it is difficult to be serious about the pursuit of peace and at the same time indifferent to acts that challenge it. Yet, even this may be too controversial for the IOC. As Reeve (2000) describes in relation to the Munich 1972 assault on the Israeli team,

> The West typically views such barbarous attacks with disgust, and the perpetrators as 'evil terrorists.' But the roots of the anger and frustration that gave birth to Black September, and led to the ... attack in Munich, run deep, back through centuries, to the very heart of the dispute between the Israelis and the Palestinians. It is impossible to comprehend ... the desperation of the Munich attackers without understanding the tragic history of both sides.
>
> (Reeve 2000: 22)

In this sense, passing any kind of judgements over entrenched political conflicts may be a high risk for the Olympic movement. As such, Rogge's refusal to comment was appropriate, but, we argue, not for the reason that he gave. The Olympics are a politically engaged movement and the actions of the IOC reveal a clear commitment to addressing and taking a stance on certain aspects of political culture. However, this commitment stops short of aligning itself with political ideologies that would compromise its commitment to embracing as many countries as possible to compete in the Olympic

Games. Instead, it may be more credible to argue that the Olympic movement is a community whose work is politicized on numerous levels and is affected by political processes that are beyond its control. However, it is precisely for this reason that the Olympics *cannot* be regarded as separate from politics. Indeed, the Olympics may be understood historically as an organization whose work is intimately connected to political interventions.

Thus, the credibility of the claim that the Olympics are above politics does not withstand scrutiny. Certainly, its relationship to politics is complicated and has changed over time, making it very difficult to claim that there has even been a clear, singular approach to politics over the course of the modern Games. Yet, we argue that Olympism is an ideology that has clear alignment with the values of some, rather than all nations, making it an inherently political project. These values are defined principally by the Western philosophical origins of the modern Games and are aligned with broadly humanitarian aspirations, the rise of human rights and the values of international organizations. The IOC's relationship with the UN is one example of this, as we have indicated. Equally, the Olympics foster the universalizing of these beliefs, by requiring their 205 member countries to uphold the Olympic Charter which includes promoting non-discrimination and respect for human dignity.

While organizations like the IOC may be among the best placed within society to leverage governments to act towards global political development, it must find a careful balance in how it involves itself with domestic political matters. The way of addressing this challenge for the IOC has been to emphasize the role of sport within diplomatic negotiations. For example, UN Secretary General Ban-Ki Moon notes that:

> Three years ago, when the United Nations helped to organize the Democratic Republic of the Congo's first elections in 45 years, the IOC teamed up with peacekeepers to hold 'Peace Games' that helped promote calm. I thank President Rogge for backing these sports-for-peace initiatives.
>
> (Ban-Ki Moon 2009)

Alternatively, in May 2011, the IOC distributed a press release detailing its joint talks with Israeli and Palestinian leaders, to find common ground in their peaceful participation in sport. IOC President Jacques Rogge said: 'The IOC has an obligation to support measures to protect athletes and to use sport as a tool for peace and development' (IOC 2011a). Yet, while it is appealing to think of such actions as simply acts of sport development, they are also acts of developing political reconciliation in a broader sense. Indeed, this broader project of the sports field as a political arena further reinforces the idea that the Olympic movement is persistently grappling with difficult and sometimes compromising political matters, regardless of how it sees itself.

5

ETHICS AND VALUES

Political matters are often underpinned by a number of moral and ethical concerns and, in the case of the Olympics, this is no exception. For example, before deciding to bid for an Olympic Games, a society may need to consider the legitimacy of curtailed privacy and freedom, which often ensues over a Games hosting period. Alternatively, it may need to evaluate the merit of investing public funds in hosting a mega-event, when so many other social problems are in need of immediate investment. It may also need to consider such policies as the pricing of tickets for events, which could be unaffordable to many people, if maximizing profit is the main ambition, or, more importantly, housing relocation policies, which can affect large numbers of people in the trajectory towards hosting a Games. Clearly, the Olympic Games do not take place in isolation from other social affairs and it is necessary to contextualize what happens at the Olympics within broader processes of moral discourse and action. For example, the success of the Beijing 2008 Games occurred against a backdrop of both China's rise as an economic superpower and the Western credit crunch, which crippled parts of the global economy, revealing excessive corporate bonuses, government borrowing spiralling out of control and unscrupulous practices within the money markets. Moreover, these Games provoked international concerns about exploitative labour conditions, while protests occurred around the world over China's disregard for individual human rights, its role in Darfur and its occupation of Tibet. On these matters, many lobby groups argued that, rather than improve the situation, the Olympic Games exacerbated government-induced injustices, calling for ethical reform. Beijing is not unique in this regard, as we saw earlier how concerns about social justice have been apparent at numerous other Games, including Vancouver 2010, London 2012 and Rio 2016.

Regardless of the position one takes on these matters, we may regard the Olympic Games as an inherently moral enterprise with unique global dimensions. Moreover, as institutional transparency and accountability have become dominant public expectations, so too have institutions like the IOC been required to demonstrate that they are mindful of their ethical responsibilities and proactive in responding to them (Griseri and Seppala 2010). Around the turn of the millennium, this trend affected the IOC directly, as allegations of corruption were made towards its members in relation to the bidding process for the Salt Lake City 2002 Olympic Winter Games.

Over the same period, the development of new technologies forced societies to confront new moral dilemmas about the future of human civilization. In particular, the rise of the Internet, the realization of the Human Genome project and debates about climate change have each raised questions about humanity's place in the world. These events have created new ethical considerations for society, to which the Olympic movement has not been immune. Thus, the rise of new media has transformed the way in which fans consume the Olympic Games and may yet threaten the Olympic movement's economic foundation, due to the way in which it is expanding what it means to be a journalist and how media content is shared and monetized (Miah and Jones 2012). Millions of bloggers and semi-professional multimedia experts now have the capacity to generate broadcast quality output at the Games and, if this content stands to jeopardize the privileges afforded to the rights-paying mass media's, then a new economic model may be needed for the Olympic movement. Equally, progress in biotechnology has had a number of consequences for the Olympics. In support of elite sport, this new science is providing new insights to help understand the impact of elite sports performances on the health of athletes, while providing more effective therapies for athletes who are injured. Yet, some scientists have also identified a prospective era of gene doping, which could jeopardize the aspirations of the anti-doping movement irrevocably, calling for a new way of thinking about the ethics of performance enhancement in sport (Miah 2004). Alternatively, genetic testing may select out certain kinds of people before they even begin to try new sports, or may be used as a way of ensuring that sports clubs do not take high risks on athletes who have unfavourable genetic profiles.

Finally, concerns about the environment have become a core dimension of the Olympic programme and IOC activity, not least because the Games have a significant impact on a city's environment. Over the years, the legacy of these impacts has often been negative for a host city, as was the case for the Montreal 1976 Games, which became an enduring, unsustainable economic burden for the population for years after the Games had finished. Payne explains that:

> The original cost of hosting the Montreal Games was estimated at $310 million. But cost overruns on the construction of Montreal's Olympic stadium left the city burdened with debts of $1 billion. By the time these are cleared in 2006, the final cost will be about $2 billion.
>
> (Payne 2006: 9)

These trajectories have brought into focus the importance of addressing ethical issues in the Olympic movement and this chapter focuses on some specific ethical themes that have concerned the Olympics over its lifetime. We argue that the Olympics highlight a number of broad societal concerns about justice and ethics and that the importance of these to future Games hosts will continue to grow. Moreover, the Olympic Games' unique global context makes the negotiation of these ethical matters all the more difficult to resolve, since they will require the agreement of many countries, each of which have their own ethical perspectives and belief systems. The main part of our discussion focuses on three key areas of ethical concern: first, the allegations of corruption made about IOC members, notably around the Salt Lake City 2002 election process; second, anti-doping and the ethics of performance enhancement, and finally the rise of environmental ethics. While these three areas do not fully describe the range of ethical issues that are pertinent to the Olympic movement today, they represent some of the most important issues, each of which require immediate prioritization. Indeed, their importance is highlighted within the Olympic Charter, which defines the commitment of the Olympic movement to a series of such fundamental ethical issues.

These concerns about ethical conduct are also made manifest in the way that the IOC discusses the 'values of Olympism' (IOC 2010a), which involve the promotion of fair play, respect, friendship and the pursuit of excellence (see IOC 2007). Critics of the Olympic movement have noted that there is a contradiction in how the IOC develops educational material like this around the concept of Olympism, when it might equally hold in high esteem the values of corporate culture and commercial ownership, as recognizable features of the Olympic programme. It is in the context of these dualities that our ethical analysis is framed.

CORRUPTION AND REFORM

It may be because of the high political stakes of the Olympics or the sheer amount of money involved in their staging, but the organization of the Games in modern times has been accompanied by periodic allegations of corruption directed towards various actors within the Olympic movement (Simson and Jennings 1992, Jennings 1996). The scale of these allegations ranges from mildly disgruntled public objections to the way in which Olympic sponsors receive large amounts of tickets at the Games as part of their corporate package, to allegations of corruption directed towards IOC members and OCOG staff. In 1992, British journalist Andrew Jennings published *The Lords of the Rings*, later republished as *The New Lords of the Rings* (1996), which detailed allegations of bribery including the offering of gifts and privileges to IOC members in exchange for votes. Six years later, after endless campaigning over the issues, the world's media and public scrutiny was directed towards the Salt Lake City 2002 Olympic Winter Games, when many such allegations came to light. Mallon (2000: 11) describes what happened when, on 24 November 1998, the IOC was thrown into turmoil:

> the Salt Lake City (Utah) television station, KTVX, reported that the Salt Lake Olympic Organizing Committee for the Olympic Winter Games of

2002 (SLOC) had been paying for Sonia Essomba to attend the American University in Washington. The announcement by itself seemed innocent enough, but it had far reaching repercussions, and what eventually transpired threatened the entire existence of the International Olympic Committee. Sonia Essomba was the daughter of René Essomba, the late IOC member (1978–98) to Cameroon. The payments, it would be revealed, were part of a larger scheme set up by SLOC to award scholarships to the family members and friends of IOC members in an effort to win their votes to become the Host City.

The most decorated IOC member of this period to be subject to these allegations was Republic of Korea's Un Yong Kim, who received a 'most severe warning' from the IOC following the Salt Lake City 2002 bid case. While this was not enough to prevent him from coming second in the IOC Presidential election of 2001, he was subsequently ejected from the IOC in 2004, following criminal prosecutions of embezzlement and bribery by Korean courts (IOC 2005b).

Allegations of corruption are not unique to the Olympics. In 2011 similar concerns were expressed about lack of transparency within FIFA over decisions to award the World Cup to Russia in 2018 and Qatar in 2022. Equally, such allegations of Olympic corruption do not extend only to IOC members, but also to members of OCOGs. Even national government ministers have been the target of such claims, when their practices for securing bids have been seen as unethical. For example, when the 2012 Olympic Games decision was made in Singapore during 2006, it was reported that British Prime Minister Tony Blair went to Singapore and staged a number of meetings with IOC members, which the newspaper *Le Monde* reported as unethical (Randall and Helm 2006). Little is known about what took place in those meetings and this is partly why they were seen as problematic, given their proximity to the vote.

As a result of the bid process corruption allegations in the 1990s, the IOC was compelled to create a Reform Commission, which reported to the IOC General Assembly in December 1999 (IOC 1999). The terms of reference for this eighty-two-member committee were broadly about how the IOC operates, including its composition, role and, notably, the 'designation of Olympic Games Host cities' (ibid.). Among the recommendations were a maximum length of term for the IOC President, a reduced age limit from 80 to 70 for IOC members who were appointed after 1999, and a contractual requirement for Olympic host cities also to stage the Paralympic Games. However, the most salient recommendations concerned the bid process and, particularly, the interaction of IOC members with bid city leaders. For example, the Commission recommended that it should not be necessary for IOC members to visit candidate cities but that, where an IOC member feels this to be important in making a decision about a bid, the IOC 'Executive Board will decide under which conditions the visit(s) can take place and the IOC Administration will organize and cover the costs of such visit(s)' (IOC 1999: 29).

The adoption of these measures was overseen by the newly established Ethics Commission (also a consequence of the reform), which consisted of high-ranking IOC members – President and Vice Presidents. Moreover, a significant part of its early work involved establishing a Code of Ethics (IOC 2009c) that would govern the activity of IOC members, particularly in relation to its contact with bid cities. Since the 2000 reforms, every inter-action between an IOC member and a bid city is now logged and bid cities are under strict rules governing their conduct with IOC members. Moreover, the Code of Ethics defines all obligations of the IOC and its partners to uphold prescribed ethical principles, which apply to all parts of the Olympic family, from an OCOG through to individual participants – which include athletes, officials, media and any person accredited by the IOC to attend the Olympic Games.

There are many other partners within the Olympic movement whose activities may also be subject to ethical scrutiny – or, at least, one may wish them to be. While the IOC Code of Ethics does not apply formally to the major sponsors that contribute to the financial stability of the Olympic movement, it makes provisions for ensur-ing that the Olympic activity of these organizations is consistent with the Olympic values. Thus, within the Code of Ethics, it states that:

> [the support that] broadcasters, sponsors, partners and other suppor-ters make to the development and prestige of the Olympic Games ...

must be in a form consistent with the rules of sport and the principles defined in the Olympic Charter and the present Code.

(IOC 2009c: 86)

As such, any Olympic partner may be held to the IOC's ethical agenda when developing its Olympic Games programme. One crucial aspect of such collaboration in recent years has been in the area of environmental sustainability, the second major ethical issue facing the Olympics today.

ENVIRONMENT AND SUSTAINABILITY

As for many organizations that rely on corporate sponsorship to survive, the Olympics may be criticized for having commercialized the value of their great symbol by selling the rings to transnational corporations, which, in turn, may have compromised the Olympics' integrity as a social movement (MacAloon 2011). Yet, the IOC would defend this decision by drawing attention to their financial vulnerability before these agreements were put in place, a situation which threatened the survival of the modern Olympic Games. As Payne writes:

More and more Olympic observers admit that this tension is no longer a conflictual one, but rather a dynamic balance where the identity of the Olympics, as the embodiment of a special set of values, engages in a delicate dance with commercial entities eager to use that identity to sell products.

(Payne 2006: 17)

However, a third interpretation of his relationship is that the association between these organizations and the Olympic movement compels the former to adopt codes of practice and values that they otherwise would be slower to adopt. Thus, in the context of environmental concerns, we may examine how the Olympics influences the work of its partners to produce an ethically conscientious Olympic Games. Of course, one may argue that a resolute commitment to the environment would mean that the Olympic Games should not happen at all or, if they did, they certainly ought to happen in the same place every time to ensure minimal environmental impact, which is created by the construction of new venues and infrastructural change. Yet, herein lies the challenge, as such strong commitments to avoid environmental damage means that humanity must choose which kinds of lifestyles are morally tenable and how environmental impacts are offset by advancements in other social areas.

So prominent have ethical concerns about the environment become within IOC literature that it is now sometimes referred to as the third pillar of Olympism (Cantelon 1999), where the other two are sport and culture (IOC 2002a, Maslova 2010).[1] Indeed, within their bid presentations for the 2018 Olympic Winter Games, each of the finalists – Annecy, Munich and PyeongChang – highlighted their commitment to ensuring that their Games would be the first carbon-neutral Games. The origins of environmental concern within the IOC derive from the United Nations' 'Agenda 21', a consequence of the 1992 Rio de Janeiro Earth Summit. Agenda 21 sets out a number of aspirations for environmental sustainability encompassing such areas as deforestation, biodiversity, atmospheric obligations and industrial development. At the time, the growing sense that the Olympic Games have a dramatic environmental impact on a host city created considerable pressure on the Olympic movement to prioritize sustainability targets within bids. In 1995, the IOC formed a *Sport and Environment Commission*, which began to work closely with the UNEP and made its commitment explicit in the Olympic Charter in 1996, which states that the IOC's role is to ensure

> that the Olympic Games are held in conditions which demonstrate a responsible concern for environmental issues and [the IOC should ensure that it] encourages the Olympic Movement to demonstrate a responsible concern for environmental issues, takes measures to reflect such concern in its activities and educates all those connected with the Olympic Movement as to the importance of sustainable development.
>
> (IOC 1996: 10)

In 1999, the IOC adopted the overarching Agenda 21 objectives (IOC, no date). This led to creating a *Manual on Sport and the Environment* (IOC 2005c) directed towards all participants in the Olympic movement. Today, the IOC Evaluation Commission also has 'environment' as a key dimension of scrutiny within a bid city's application. The most recent version of the Charter reads only slightly differently from the original amendment, indicating the IOC's role is 'to encourage and support a responsible concern for environmental issues, to promote sustainable development in sport and to require that the Olympic Games are held accordingly' (IOC 2010a). Moreover, this obligation is now written into the host city contract with the IOC. In the case of Athens 2004, it states that

> The city and the HOC (Hellenic Olympic Committee) recognize and agree that the respect of the environment is an important issue and undertake the responsibility to fulfill their obligations and activities as these stem from the present contract, in a way that adopts the principle of Sustainable Development, respects the relevant environmental legislation and, wherever possible, promotes the protection of the environment.
>
> (Chapter II, article 18, Contract between the IOC and the host city of Athens, cited in World Wildlife Fund 2004: 14)

Finally, the IOC Code of Ethics also includes a provision which states that:

> The Olympic parties shall endeavour to protect the environment on the occasion of any events they organise. In the context of the Olympic Games, they undertake to uphold generally accepted standards for environmental protection.
>
> (IOC 2009c: 86)

However, the ability of the IOC to affect the overall environmental impact of the Olympic Games may be limited by the fact that its provisions are not precise enough to make it possible to enforce through the legally binding host city contract. Yet, if the host city is seen to have failed in reaching the expected standards, the IOC may impose a fine. In 2011, it has indicated that this would involve withholding '25% of the expected £700m broadcasting income generated from the Games should air quality levels exceed EU limits during the games' (Vidal and Gibson 2011).

Despite the many initiatives made by OCOGs, NOCs and sponsors to promote environmental sustainability in all of the work of the Olympic movement, the achievements of Olympic Games hosts have been somewhat mixed, which highlights one of the limitations in how the Olympic movement influences host cities in the delivery of their Olympic Games. For example, for the Athens 2004 Olympic Games, the World Wildlife Fund (WWF) evaluation of its sustainable achievements was very negative, arguing that numerous dimensions of concern were not addressed, including the protection of natural habitats, sustainable construction of venues, use of renewable energy sources, water conservation, and recycling. In its conclusion, the WWF is also critical of the provision within the host city contract over environmental protection which it claims is 'only general' (World Wildlife Fund 2004: 13). For the London 2012 contract, it is similarly general, which may indicate that present host cities are also lacking in guidance:

> The City, the NOC and the OCOG undertake to carry out their obligations and activities under this Contract in a manner which embraces the concept of environmental sustainable development, and which complies with applicable environmental legislation and serves to promote the protection of the environment. In particular, the concept of environmental sustainable development shall address concerns for the post-Olympic use of venues and other facilities and infrastructures and, in general, positive legacies in environmental practices and policies in accordance with the Olympic Charter.
>
> (IOC 2005a: 12)[2]

Beyond the construction of venues, it is also difficult to confirm whether the relationship between sponsors and the Olympics is a catalyst for a transformation in the overarching ethical practices of any corporation. It is apparent that the IOC values have evolved alongside the emergence of corporate social responsibilities but whether these values have any wider adoption outside of a sponsors' Games time activity is much harder to prove. It would seem that the various commitments made by an OCOG and the host city should influence the contracts it makes with service providers, but it is doubtful whether the expectations translate through to the final delivery. That said, stories about environmental achievements are commonplace within the OCOG's discourse about its Games' development. Moreover, sponsors undertake numerous initiatives that provide symbolic gestures towards environmental concern, such as Coca-Cola's sponsoring of recycling bins in London during the Games (see the Coca-Cola website). On the approach to Beijing 2008, BOCOG established an 'Olympic Sponsor Environment Group', which 'brought national and global sponsors together to coordinate environmental initiatives' (United Nations Environmental Programme 2009: 112). Projects included the use of a natural cooling initiative for Coca-Cola drinks to use less ozone depleting hydrofluorocarbons, the installation of eco-friendly air conditioning in Olympic venues and environmentally friendly mobile phones for Olympic family members.

Yet, there is a contradiction between this work and the fact that many Olympic sponsors are also among the most prominent targets of environmental campaigners, which has drawn attention to the failure of these corporations to live up to their social responsibilities. For example, in 2006 Greenpeace criticized long-term Olympic partner McDonalds for its role in the deforestation of the Amazon. By drawing attention to its reliance on soya products for chicken feed that would eventually be used in the creation of Chicken McNuggets, Greenpeace mobilized the fast-food restaurant in developing a campaign against using soya in the industry (Greenpeace 2006). Another major long-term partner, Coca-Cola, is also caught up in numerous campaigns, despite the fact that it continuously highlights its contributions to environmental sustainability throughout its PR material.

Even companies with the most spectacularly bad ethical track records on environmental concerns may become part of an Olympic programme, as is the case of British Petroleum and the London 2012 Games. Despite what happened with Deep Water Horizon in 2010, there was never any suggestion that BP would cease to be a Premier Partner of the London 2012 Games. Clearly, there is a lot more that these organizations could be doing to make the Games more ethically engaged. Indeed, the UNEP acknowledges that the IOC needs to 'formalize' the sponsors' contribution to the Olympic environmental sustainability programme, rather than rely solely on OCOG-led initiatives, along with measures of indicators of success, such as public awareness or comparative scales against which host cities may be evaluated. Yet, the UNEP also notes that the Olympic movement's commitment to such principles is not common among all mega-events and that it should therefore be commended for making it such a priority: 'For example, Official Partners of the FIFA World Cup are not assessed on the basis of their environmental performance' (United Nations Environmental Programme 2009: 114).

There may also be a broader set of issues at stake with regard to sustainability than just environmental protection when considering the Olympics. First, it is necessary to recognize that not all countries are able to support a singular universal standard, when their infrastructure or economy is not ready to meet such expectations. Thus, environmental targets must be sensitive to national differences with regard to the available technology and resources. The UNEP Independent Environmental Assessment (United Nations Environmental Programme 2009) of the Beijing 2008 Games indicated that it invested over $17 billion in environmental projects over the Olympic period, but this kind of investment is unlikely to be available to many host cities. Second, sustainability may need a wider definition than it presently enjoys within Olympic debates, as exemplified by Hawkes' (2001) notion of environmental sustainability through cultural change. Hawkes draws attention to the fact that behavioural shifts are as much tied to the cultural ecology of a population as they are associated with the ethical actions taken by various sectors of society.

Despite the commitments to environmental sustainability made by the IOC, the Olympic Games is an event that has a dramatic environmental impact on a city. Indeed, at recent Games, so extensive are the interventions on the environment that even 'weather modification' is an increasingly established part of what a city is prepared to undertake to ensure the successful running of the Games. For instance, at the Beijing 2008 Games, the city's 'Weather Modification Office' undertook an increasingly established practice of 'cloud seeding' in advance of the Games to promote rainfall, with the intention of reducing the levels of pollution experienced by athletes during the competition fortnight. While the scientific evidence to support the effectiveness of this practice is unclear, it reveals a fundamental tension in how we make sense of pursuing sustainability when discussing the Olympic Games.

To this end, the responsible action in the future may be to conclude that the Olympics – and, indeed, the staging of elite sports – may not be feasible in a world with such limited natural resources. Of course, the balance here is in society deciding what it feels are reasonable human pursuits to undertake, in order to give life meaning and value and this is a debate that will go on for years to come. While it may be unreasonable to expect too much from the relationship between the Olympic movement and its corporate partners, it is apparent that the adoption of sustainable policies around the Games shows how its environmental impact has begun to be addressed over the years. In this sense, it may yet be too early to judge whether the Olympics has achieved all it claims to over meeting sustainability targets. Nevertheless, the increase in public awareness of environmental sustainability issues generated by the Games may be an adequate contribution to such work as a force for good in locating debates about such matters in a broader political agenda.

DOPING AND HUMAN ENHANCEMENT

We conclude our overview of ethical issues with reference to perhaps the most publicly charged ethical debate in the Olympics today, that of doping. One of the defining features of contemporary Olympic competition has been its struggle against doping in elite sport, the pursuit of which occupies the agendas of all elite sports organizations today. In the same way as concerns about the environment, doping is another dimension of the Olympic movement that unites it with a wide array of other institutions of global governance, such as the United Nations, the World Health Organization and various departments of national governments. It is also an issue that has received considerable investment from the IOC, though some have questioned whether this investment has been either adequate or successful. However, what elevates doping concerns above all other ethical issues surrounding the Olympics is their prominence in the global media as a thread that runs through all major sports competitions, irrespective of where the Games are taking place.

While there are many organizations involved with monitoring anti-doping today, the history of anti-doping policy-making goes back many years, almost to the birth of the modern Olympic Games. However, the IOC did not become proactive in addressing the culture of doping until a series of high-profile athlete deaths in the 1960s, including that of Knut Jenson at the Rome 1960 Olympic Games and the dramatic televised death of Tour de France cyclist Tommie Simpson in 1967 (Houlihan 1999). As for any performance-enhancing techniques, the range of banned substances used by athletes has changed over the years. Indeed, there is some evidence that the pursuit of doping goes back as far as the ancient Games, where performance-enhancing mushrooms may have been used in a similar way to modern pharmaceutical products. After the 1960s, the next defining period in anti-doping policy was the 1980s, which began with the Moscow 1980 Games, dubbed the 'Junkie Olympics' because of the prominent use of anabolic steroids. By the beginning of the 1990s, with the fall of the Berlin Wall in 1989, the new, free press of Germany revealed the extent of the systematic doping that was taking place within the East Germany sports establishment. Hoberman (1992: 224) notes how this included reports that 'children as young as twelve had been given steroids'. This realization had a dramatic impact on how the IOC responded to the doping situation.

Soon after, another scandal reached the world's attention, again at the Tour de France. After years of debate about the prevalence of doping in cycling, a series of police raids on cyclists led to a protest sit-down by cyclists in the middle of the seventeenth stage of the 1998 Tour. The following year the IOC convened the First World Conference on Doping in Sport in Lausanne, which led to the creation of the World Anti-Doping Agency (WADA) on 10 November 1999. The principal aim of WADA was to create a global standard of anti-doping policy, which became known as the Worldwide Anti-Doping Code and International Standards, implemented on 1 January 2004. While WADA began as an IOC-funded initiative, it now receives 50 per cent of its funding from national governments and operates independently of the IOC with headquarters in Montreal. However, the IOC financial contribution is based on achieving the requisite donation from the national governments (see WADA website). Since its emergence, WADA may be seen as the third most important regulatory structure within the Olympic movement, alongside the IOC Ethics Commission and the Court of Arbitration for Sport (CAS), the latter of which is also an important force in the arbitration of doping cases in elite sports. CAS is a body that was originally conceived by IOC

President Juan Antonio Samaranch in 1983 and also initially funded by the IOC until 1994, after which its annual funding of around $9m derived from Olympic television rights sales (CAS website). In addition to overseeing doping cases, CAS is also utilized in disputes among members of the Olympic family and rule challenges in sport (Blackshaw 2003).

This brief historical overview of the anti-doping movement helps to situate the breadth of organizations whose work is implicated within such projects, not least of which are government and inter-governmental bodies, such as the European Union. Indeed, given how widespread the support for anti-doping is across the social and political sphere, it may seem counter-intuitive to present doping as an ethical dilemma for the Olympic movement at all. After all, if everybody agrees that doping is wrong, then there is no funda-mental ethical question to answer. That is, of course, unless everyone is wrong, or that their way of addressing the problem is logically flawed. In the case of the latter, one may argue that a system of anti-doping testing which requires testing children in schools is evidence of an ethical system gone wrong, or at the very least a system that is prepared to go to any lengths to protect the so-called level playing field of elite sport. The problem may be compared to debates about the existence of climate change today, which in many political spheres is a discussion that no longer takes place because challenging its existence has been rejected so strongly. Similarly, within the world of sport, challenging the belief that doping is wrong and should be stopped is largely unheard of and certainly not a position that any practising athlete or sports official would be willing to articulate in public.

Yet, there *is* evidence of doubt over whether the pursuit of anti-doping is morally justified. For example, the American Academy of Pediatrics (2005) argues that the work of anti-doping does not address the wider culture of body modification that exists in American society. Alternatively, Kayser, Mauron and Miah (2007) claim that the current model of test, detect and disqualify is ineffective in both catching cheats and deterring the use of illicit substances, arguing that instead a harm reduction model of supervised doping would be preferable. Furthermore, it is clear that there are some doping-like technologies over which the Olympic movement is relatively ambivalent, such as altitude chambers which change the density of oxygen within the atmosphere thus enhancing athletic endurance. Indeed, it is examples like this that are the focus of the broader point we wish to highlight, which is that methods of doping are just one end of a spectrum of technologies that are changing the athlete's performance within the Olympics today. Thus, today's anti-doping movement cannot be isolated from broader processes of technologization that are changing societies, altering humanity and taking Olympic competition into a brave new world of human enhancement. For some, this trajectory further removes the Olympic Games from Coubertin's vision for sport, which was founded on the principles of amateurism (Hoberman 1992). For others, twenty-first-century sport is made meaningful by the democratization of technology, which has made possible mass participation in sports through affordable sports technologies. Yet, it is also a period defined by the biotechnology industries, which have opened up the possibility of regarding the human species as an unfinished biological entity in need of modification to deal with the stress and strain of specialist human tasks, like athletic competition.

These two eras of elite sport are united by the common Olympic value of pursuing 'excellence'; the difficulty is that they embody different interpretations of this term. For the former, technology compromises and overshadows the natural achievements of athletes, though at times it allows for a more representative appraisal of ability. For the latter, technology makes sport possible and its continued development makes competition even more exciting to undertake and witness.

These trends towards enhancement are not unique to the Olympics. Rather, a wide range of enhancement technologies is rapidly becoming available for people to use outside sport, in work or leisure (United States President's Council on Bioethics 2003). In this context of biotechnological modifications, one may ask whether WADA will still have a role to play in an era when non-athletes are modifying themselves through numerous forms of technology. Indeed, will anybody care if an athlete has used a drug to enhance performance, when such lifestyle modifications are commonplace within society?

Furthermore, drugs may be the least problematic example of performance enhancements for future Olympic Games, as an array of bionic prosthetic devices become a seamless part of human biology. For example, on the approach to the Beijing 2008 Olympic Games, the double below-the-knee amputee and Paralympic champion Oscar Pistorius campaigned for his right to take part in the Olympics, rather than just the Paralympics. Yet, there was considerable controversy over whether his prosthetic 'cheetah foot' would give him an advantage over other competitors – a proposition that transforms the idea that being able-bodied is the optimal condition for sports performance. Pistorius's campaign was challenged by the overseeing sports federation, the IAAF, which amended its rules in such a way as effectively to exclude Pistorius on the basis of his prosthetic device. However, the Court of Arbitration for Sport found that this decision appeared to have been introduced specifically with Pistorius in mind and so upheld Pistorius's appeal to overturn the IAAF ruling, both on grounds of discrimination and arguing that evidence of his advantage was not convincing. Unfortunately, despite having the IAAF decision overturned, Pistorius was just short of the qualifying time, so was unable to compete in the Olympic Games. Yet, it remains possible that, in a future Games, the challenge from Paralympians to the Olympic athlete will arise again.

In any case, what if Pistorius's legs do provide an advantage over their biological counterparts? Does this make it unfair or is this unfairness morally significant? One of the central questions to face the Olympic Games in this area is whether it is able to distinguish between legitimate inequalities in sport. Even within able-bodied sports, there are vast differences of technological enablement at work and these variations are likely only to grow. To this end, maintaining fairness is increasingly a conviction of faith, rather than a condition that can be achieved within elite sports competition. Moreover, each individual athlete will become more strategic in finding their technology of choice in what have already become contests of technology and biology. However, there is a broader point at stake in this case. As intimated earlier, deciding whether Pistorius should compete as an Olympian or a Paralympian is not so much a problem of whether he is competing in a different type of event. Rather, his campaign exposes the injustice of separation that occurs between the Olympic and Paralympic programme and, arguably, the significance of this far exceeds that of ensuring fairness for the present, temporary population of able-bodied athletes. Thus, the question we should be asking is not whether Paralympians should compete at the Olympics, but why they are separate in the first place. There is nothing within the Olympic Charter that requires the separation of these two sets of competitions, it is just a fact of their different histories. However, if Coubertin had conceived the Olympic Games today, where disabilities discrimination legislation abounds, it is hard to imagine that the world would have two separate Games.

Finally, one might argue that one of the central values of elite performance practices, such as sport, music, or dance, is the demonstrable capacity to extend what has been previously assumed to be the limits of humanity. If society expects individuals to break world records or extend creative insights, then technologies that transcend mere optimization of human capacities will become a necessity. In the near future, we might not see the engineering of pianists with six fingers on each hand, as depicted in the science fiction film *GATTACA* (Niccol 1997), who are able to play divine new compositions. Yet, it is pertinent to scrutinize the moral concern that arises from such a prospect as conceptually similar achievements are already undertaken via body modification in sports. While doping has steadily changed the character of the Olympics, there remains an enduring tension in deciding whether or not technology takes athletes too far in their pursuit of excellence. No more apparent is this concern than in the debate about doping. Moreover, while the world of sport has generally always lagged behind the doping athlete in terms of having tests to detect cheating, in 2011, WADA also achieved a landmark agreement with the pharmaceutical manufacturer GlaxoSmithKline to share knowledge about emerging, pre-commercialized substances that may be utilized by athletes in the future. This agreement may change the effectiveness of anti-doping dramatically, placing WADA in a much stronger position to stay ahead of the doping athletes.

To conclude this chapter, when we look through the lens of ethics and values it becomes clear both what the Olympic movement expects to elevate as its ideals, and also that these aspirations align with broader processes of ethical debate and policy that occur outside of the Olympics, as these three cases reveal. The regulation of IOC members and other Olympic partners is now a permanent procedural feature of the IOC and certainly an indication of progress in how it is governed and audited. Yet, the role of independent bodies like the UNEP or the WWF is clearly necessary in the area of environmental sustainability to ensure that host cities aspire to the appropriate ethical targets. Finally, the concept of the ethical human in the doping debate speaks to Coubertin's aspirations for the Olympic athlete as the embodiment of physical accomplishment and intellectual enlightenment. While we noted in Chapter 1 that the Olympic motto of 'citius, altius, fortius' is not a licence to pursue the limitless excess of achievement within Olympic sport, the technologization of modern sport takes the Olympics in a direction that may have little resemblance not only to the ancient Games, but even to the sports of the twentieth century.

MANAGEMENT AND ECONOMICS

The staging of an Olympic Games may be likened to the equivalent of organizing twenty-six international sports events, ten royal weddings, three European Capital of Culture programmes, two World Expos and one World-Cup Final all at the same time and over a sixteen-day period. When the Paralympic Games are included, the work is almost doubled. Thus, the duration of the planning, the scale of the stakeholder community and the extent of reliance on public and private funds sets it apart as one of the largest undertakings that a nation may face in a peacetime setting. This makes discussions about the management and economics of the Games a vast subject with the potential to include anything from what is required to manage car parking at competition venues to attributing a country's annual security budget as a cost of staging the Olympic Games.

Yet, managing the Games is only one task of the Olympic movement. Other areas of management include involvement with such organizations as the World Anti-Doping Agency, the United Nations, the National Olympic Committees and International Sports Federations, to name just a few.[1] Numerous studies have been published on both the management and economics of the Olympics (Chappelet and Bayley 2005, Preuss 2006), so to focus our attention, we consider only aspects that have been central to the development of the Olympic movement and which provide key insights into the complexity of its economic structure over the last thirty years. First, we explore aspects of managing the Olympics, distinguishing between two key parameters – the Olympic family and the Olympic Games. Subsequently, we consider where the money comes from and where it is invested. While in Chapter 8 we discuss approaches to assessing the economic impact of an Olympic Games, here we provide key information about the management and economic infrastructure that sustains the work of the Olympic movement, taking into account what happens both within the IOC and in the organizations which work with it to deliver Olympic activities.

MANAGING THE OLYMPIC MOVEMENT

Discussions about the Olympics tend to focus on their most visible components – the Olympic Games and its prominent guardians, the Organizing Committees of the Olympic Games and the IOC. However, underpinning these elements is a network of organizations whose work extends well beyond the Games, as previous chapters have indicated. Understanding how the Games are managed and what position they occupy in the world means first coming to terms with the role of the various organizations which converge around Olympic interests and, importantly, recognizing what social, legal and political status they have around the world.

In Chapter 1, we provided an overview of how the IOC has been structured historically, the role of its President, Members, Commissions and Executive Board which drive the strategic mission of the Olympic movement. We also detailed the various dimensions of what is often referred to as the Olympic family, which encompasses International Sports Federations, National Olympic Committees (NOCs), athletes, sponsors, broadcast partners and United Nations agencies. In this chapter we discuss how different forms of management are required across each of these levels of Olympic infrastructure. For instance, an NOC will both have some formal oversight from the IOC, but will also be required to develop its own resource support from respective national governments (which are the primary source of NOC funding in Europe), and sustain relationships with its own domestic sponsors. NOCs also work in coordination with the Association of National Olympic Committees and their respective continental NOC association, such as the European Olympic Committees.

In addition to these networks, IOC members and senior executives in NOCs are also often individuals with extensive affiliations which contribute to the wider ecology of the Olympic movement. For example, numerous IOC members hold royal titles within their countries, while others have senior military or governmental positions. These examples reveal the extent of the political positions held by Olympic family members and indicate how occupying an Olympic office has historically been a role of national prestige. It also suggests how the business of the Olympics transcends sports competitions and is closely allied with broader geopolitical relationships. This may not be surprising when we take into account that the Olympic Games are the largest peacetime operation held by any country, thus requiring cooperation and collaboration with – presently – 205 nation-states. Indeed, it reveals how the Games are important symbols of a nation and of international political relationships. Understanding this broader ecology of the Olympic movement is crucial to making sense of its unique position. It is this network of relationships among its members and stakeholder organizations that shapes a number of the IOC's priorities and values.

The Olympic movement is also a network bound by the concept of *solidarity*, whereby the wealthier nations provide support to those with more limited economic means. This principle of cooperation is made manifest within the 'Olympic Solidarity' programme, which provides diverse forms of financial assistance to all NOCs. The Olympic Solidarity programme has its roots in the 1960s, emerging from the work of the IOC's Commission for Olympic Aid and the International Institute for Development (Olympic Solidarity 2006). The Committee for Olympic Solidarity was created via the merger of these two bodies and its value can be seen in the context of the rapid growth in the number of countries that received Olympic status over the 1960s, resulting in over fifty new NOCs, most of which represented developing nations (ibid.). Funds for Olympic Solidarity derive from the portion of television rights allocated to the NOCs and the amount of money available has grown along with the growth of television rights fees. From 2009 to 2012, this amounts to $311 million, which funds such activities as ensuring athletes are able to attend the Games, local coaching courses and NOC management (Olympic Solidarity 2009).

At the opposite end of the economic spectrum, the IOC is also engaged with managing relationships with its key financial stake-holders, notably the Olympic Games broadcasters and sponsors. Such relationships have been a part of the Olympic management system since their inception. For example, at the Stockholm 1912 Games, Swedish companies purchased the 'sole rights to take photographs and sell memorabilia at the Olympic Games' (IOC 2011b: 18). However, over the last thirty years, the IOC has implemented a novel marketing programme which has dramatically changed the fortunes of the Olympic movement. Principally, this is characterized by a global marketing model involving the sale of exclusive association with the Olympic programme to sponsors and broadcasters worldwide.

The primary IOC sponsorship programme is called *The Olympic Partners* (TOP) and involves four-year (quadrennium) contracts with corporations that receive the exclusive right to be associated with the Olympics over any competitor in their given product category. During the 2009-2012 quadrennium (labeled TOP VII), these partners and their appointed product categories are as follows: Coca-Cola (non-alcoholic beverages), Acer (computing technology equipment), Atos Origin (Information Technology), General Electric (Power), McDonalds (Retail Food), Omega (Timing, Scoring, Venue Results), Panasonic (AV/TV), Samsung (Wireless Communications), Dow (Official Chemistry), PandG (personal care and household products) and Visa (Consumer Payment Systems). In addition to TOP, NOCs have ongoing relationships with domestic sponsors and are tasked with creating a complementary programme of support via their appointed OCOG when hosting the Games. While OCOGs have held domestic sponsorship packages for many years in advance of the establishment of the TOP programme, they are now required to create a joint marketing strategy which respects the exclusive contract entitlements held by TOP sponsors (see IOC 2011b). Overall, some of the TOP sponsors and broadcasters have changed over the years, but there is a clear rhetoric within the IOC to develop long-term partnerships and the longest of these is with Coca-Cola, which began its sponsorship of the Games in 1928.

Despite the IOC's desire to maximize the revenue generated by broadcasters and sponsors via competitive contracts, historically, there have been conditions placed on the activity of each, which suggests the IOC's intentions to limit the dominance of commercial messages within the Games. For instance, while sponsors' presence around the Olympic city is extensive – including the creation of an Olympic Sponsors Village and exclusive use of street billboards throughout the city for the duration of the Games fortnight – Olympic venues remain free from any commercial advertising. Specifically, Rule 51.2 of the Olympic Charter notes that,

> No form of advertising or other publicity shall be allowed in and above the stadia, venues and other competition areas which are considered as part of the Olympic sites. Commercial installations and advertising signs shall not be allowed in the stadia, venues or other sports grounds.
>
> (IOC 2010a: 98)

As such, when watching the Olympics on television, viewers will never see any sponsorship or advertising beyond the Olympic symbols, except within commercial breaks or footage from the Olympic city. Additionally, the IOC has traditionally made a point of not always accepting the highest bid offer for the broadcasting of the Games, instead awarding the rights to the organization that can deliver the largest television audience. As noted in the Olympic Charter, 'the IOC takes all necessary steps in order to ensure the fullest coverage by the different media and the widest possible audience in the world for the Olympic Games' (IOC 2010a: 96). Furthermore, former IOC President Samaranch noted that,

> the reason we accepted a smaller sum from EBU than from News Corporation is that we reach a far larger audience with terrestrial channels, especially young people. That has always been our priority, rather than simply to accept the highest bidder.
>
> (Samaranch, cited in Payne 2006: 54)

This has maximized the number of free-to-air viewing hours for Olympic fans and explains the long-term role of such organizations as the European Broadcasting Union (EBU) which, since 1956, guaranteed broadcasting rights to many publicly funded national broadcasters such as the BBC in the UK or TVE in Spain. However, it is important to recognize how relatively recent these arrangements are and how fragile the principles may be. Thus, the commitment to maximizing free-to-air viewing hours may be in jeopardy as the escalating fees attached to the Olympic Games make it increasingly difficult for public service broadcasters to compete with private bids. Indeed, for the Sochi 2014 and Rio 2016 Games, the EBU was outbid for the first time in fifty years by the private organization SportFive, perhaps suggesting a new era of pay-per-view Olympic broadcasting (Holmwood 2008). While the IOC may defend this development by arguing that it will still give rise to a wider audience, if that audience is able to see only 200 hours of free live coverage – as is suggested – then this means the majority of the audience will not see much more than the 138 hours of coverage that were broadcast at the 1936 Olympic Games (see the Olympic Broadcasting Services website), unless they are prepared to pay.

MANAGING THE OLYMPIC GAMES

THE ROLE OF THE IOC

The initial route for the IOC's management of the Olympic Games is through the bid process, which it oversees under the governance of the Olympic Charter. Bid cities must first be nominated by their respective NOC as an 'applicant city', the merit of which is then assessed by the IOC Executive Board. If shortlisted, the city reaches the status of candidate at which point – since the 2000 reform – the IOC Executive Board appoints an 'Evaluation Commission', which is tasked with undertaking visits to candidate cities and producing regular summary reports that are used to inform the IOC members' final voting decision. Each stage has precise guidelines and rules restricting the work of each city at specific points in time. For example, applicant cities are not permitted to use the Olympic symbol within their emblem design, while candidate cities are expected to include it (IOC 2009a). All applicant cities must complete an IOC questionnaire which is presently divided into eleven primary areas: Vision, concept and legacy; Sport and venues; Environment and meteorology; Accommodation; Transport; Medical services and doping control; Safety and security; Technology and energy; Legal aspects and customs and immigration formalities; Government and public support; Finance and marketing (IOC 2011c). Those cities that become candidates must complete extended versions of the questionnaire and produce a final bid report. Once the city's bid is submitted, candidate cities are then asked to make a formal presentation within the IOC Session (the annual general meeting of all IOC members) when IOC members vote on who will win.

Once a host city is selected, its leaders along with the NOC sign a host city contract with the IOC and appoint an Organizing Committee for the Olympic Games (OCOG). This is the point at which the Games hosting process begins, lasting a total of seven years from the point of awarding the Games to their eventual delivery. Throughout this process, most IOC departments have some involvement with the organization of the Games, providing guidance or demanding information, though there are a number of key areas which have an especially important role. In particular, the 'Coordination Commission' monitors and assists the OCOG in its delivery of the Games (IOC 2010a: 77). This Commission is also responsible for ensuring that the OCOG adheres to the Olympic Charter and specifications of the IOC host city contract.

To assist the bidding and hosting process, the IOC provides extensive guidelines in the form of technical manuals, which encompass the general rules of hosting the Games, but also detailed information about specific dimensions. Current available manuals cover the areas of: Designs Standards, Sport, Olympic Village, Transport, Media, Ticketing, Brand Protection, Marketing Partner Services, Protocol, Workforce, Medical Services, Ceremonies, Communications, Games Management, Paralympic Games, IOC Session, Arrivals and Departures, City Activities, Food Services, Information Management, NOC Services, Olympic Games Impact, Olympic torch relay, Signage, Venues, OCOG Marketing, Hospitality and Visual Brand Presentation (IOC 2009a). Technical manuals are the vehicle for the IOC to outline its expectations from the OCOG. These expectations may range from broad guidelines to very specific requests. For example, the technical manual on communications (IOC 2005d)[2] conveys the IOC's interest in overseeing the OCOG's communications strategy. More precisely, the manual emphasizes Games time communications, sensitivity to different communication platforms, crisis communications and coherence with the Paralympic Games (ibid.).

Closely allied to the coordination of OCOG activities is the IOC's oversight of media activity, driven by its Commissions for

Press and for Radio and Television, which advise on how to provide the best working conditions for journalists and broadcasters. While the OCOG's role is to ensure the smooth running of media operations and provision of services during the Games, the IOC oversees important overarching dimensions that transfer from one Games to the next, such as the rules governing the media's work at the Games and the specifications of all officially accredited media centres, such as the Main Press Centre, the International Broadcasting Centre, specific venue media centres and other facilities at the Media Village (the main residence for accredited journalists). This includes a wide range of details from providing lockers with two keys for all photographers at Venue Media Centres, to ensuring adequate space at each venue. Moreover, since 2001, the IOC oversees the official Olympic Broadcasting Services (OBS), which is the production company that is employed during the Games to provide the international live feeds for all paying broadcasters.

The final area that the IOC oversees in relation to the Games is the Olympic Games Knowledge Management (OGKM) programme and Olympic Games Impact (OGI) study. Each of these elements emerged in the context of the IOC Reform Commission report (1999) and the Olympic Games Study Commission (Pound 2003), which emphasized the importance of the IOC's role in limiting the risk of OCOGs when staging the Games and taking greater responsibility in measuring the impact of an Olympic Games, an agenda that emerged particularly in the context of environmental risks. We consider these programmes in more detail in Chapter 8.

THE ROLE OF THE OCOG AND HOST CITY

It is important to understand that there is no single body responsible for delivering the Olympic Games. While the host city contract is made between the IOC and the combined responsibilities of the host city and NOC, the financial responsibility for the Games rests solely with the city and the OCOG (IOC 2010a: 76). Each host city establishes its own unique management structure within these parameters, often utilizing an additional organization to develop infrastructure and venues. For instance, for London 2012, the primary delivery organizations are the London Organizing Committee for the Olympic Games (LOCOG) and the Olympic Delivery

Authority (ODA). LOCOG is a limited company, responsible for 'staging' the Games, while the ODA is 'the public body responsible for developing and building the new venues and infrastructure for the Games and their use after 2012' (ODA website). The ODA was constituted through the London 2012 Olympic and Paralympic Games Act (2006) and is accountable to the British Government, the Greater London Authority, and other domestic host stakeholders. In contrast, LOCOG is directly accountable to the IOC and the International Paralympic Committee. In this example, we see a model that the IOC has begun to favour in recent years, whereby there is a joint responsibility taken for the Games between the host city and the OCOG in particular.

The OCOG is a very unusual company, which begins with just a few staff members at the point of initiation, grows to a few thousand by the time the Games begin, and drops again to a fraction of that number just weeks after the closing ceremony. It is a high-velocity organization with a dynamic management structure and a short life. Both the OCOG and the host city are under two primary pressures: time and money. With only seven years to organize the Games and no possibility of a delay, these organizations must coordinate numerous agencies within local and national government as well as international Olympic stakeholders (from the IOC to respective International Federations) to ensure their successful delivery in a very short space of time. Also within that period, it is necessary to raise considerable funds to offset the operational costs of the OCOG and attempt to ensure that the overall economic impact of the Games provides a favourable return on the host nation's investment. Indeed, the extensive amounts of public funds required to stage the Games means that questions about economic requirements are paramount in the host political agenda.

Previous Games have shown that success requires a seamless collaboration across these four principal management structures – IOC, NOC, host city and OCOG. Of course, within each of these stakeholders, there is a need to oversee the expectations of and potential conflicts that may arise from the tension created by the changes that are necessary to make way for the Olympics. In part, this is why recent Games have established independent legacy-focused organizations, as we discuss in Chapter 8.

ECONOMICS

There are two primary ways to discuss the economic dimensions of the Olympics – at the level of the movement or at the level of the Games, each of which requires an examination of various sources of financial accounts. For example, while the IOC's financial reports reflect elements of both movement and Games, they do not provide the full picture of the income generated by the Organizing Committee, particularly in terms of the public investment required to stage the Games. Equally, assessing the accounts of the OCOG or even the national government's contributions to the Games is still only a partial picture of how much economic investment occurs around the Olympics. For example, any individual Olympic sponsor may make a fixed contribution to the IOC as part of its quadrennial contract, but it may also undertake additional marketing programmes to maximize the privilege. On the approach to London 2012, one such activity was developed by the financial sponsor LloydsTSB and involved a mock torch relay in 2011. A prototype of the 2012 torch was taken to key sites around the UK, staging photo opportunities, as part of a campaign to select a proportion of the 2012 Olympic torch bearers. Such a project benefits from the 2012 affiliation but, like many services within the Olympic programme, involves additional financial investment from the sponsor to realize. Indeed, in many cases, paying for the privilege of being an Olympic sponsor or broadcaster may be seen as just the beginning of the total financial investment that an organization will make in order to leverage the opportunity.

Yet, perhaps the most important economic contribution to the Olympic movement is made without any remuneration, through the time and personal investment made by an athlete's family in order to enable him or her to compete at the Olympic Games. Indeed, it is the apparent contradiction between these personal investments of people with limited means and the vast amounts of money generated by the IOC contracts that often causes controversy over the way in which the Olympic economic environment is managed. It is the reliance on altruistic dedication to the Olympics that is its biggest economic asset – a point which, as some critics have noted, explains why the IOC trades on its ideals so much. The same case applies to the Olympic Games' volunteers programme, which is expected to attract up to 70,000 people for London 2012. At the Torino 2006 Olympic Winter Games, 18,000 volunteers were utilized while 45,000 applied for the roles (IOC 2006b). Famously, Beijing created positions for 100,000 volunteers – out of 1 million applications (IOC 2010b: 36). If the OCOG or IOC were required to pay the staffing costs of this community, the Games would be financially untenable. While one may argue that this system is exploitative, given that the Games bring considerable financial benefit to profit making sponsors, the altruistic act of volunteering has been a common feature of sports and other cultural events for decades and may be explained by what Titmuss (1977) would describe as a 'gift relationship', whereby the meaning of the act is defined in part by the absence of monetary reward. On this basis, one may argue that paying volunteers for their contribution to the Olympic Games would impoverish their experiences and diminish the worth of the Games. Indeed, Moreno et al. (1999) outline that key motivations for volunteering at the Games are such factors as 'The spirit of solidarity and peace enshrined in the Olympic philosophy ... Individual challenge ... [and] Belonging to a group', reinforcing the idea that what matters to the volunteer is not being paid. Alternatively, there is also evidence to show that volunteer experiences can be valuable for the development of other transferable skills which may help advance a person's career.

The financial value of investments that now circulate around the Olympic movement is substantial, but this is a relatively recent phenomenon within the IOC's history. Indeed, as Payne (2006) notes, 'At the time of Samaranch's election to the presidency [in 1980], the IOC had less than $200,000 in liquidity, and just $2 million in assets' (Payne 2006: 9). He goes on to say that 'The IOC was as inept at generating money as it was at looking after it' (Payne 2006: 12). Preuss (2006) identifies three clear periods in the Olympic movement's economic conditions: 1896–1968 – characterized by financial difficulties; 1969–80 – characterized by the growth of new revenue streams through television and sponsorship; 1981–2003 – characterized by over-commercialization and corruption. He adds a further period emerging from 2004–8, which may now be seen as a period of further commercial growth, focused on the consolidation of Olympic sponsor partnerships and the continuing rise of multi-Games broadcast contracts, but framed also by greater transparency and accountability. Thus, today's Olympic movement is remarkably different from how it operated before the 1980s. In just thirty years, the IOC has succeeded in monetizing the Olympic symbol, transforming it into one of the world's most recognized and lucrative brands:

> The results of a survey carried out in six countries (Australia, Germany, India, Japan, Great Britain and the USA) in 1995 showed that 92% of those questioned correctly identified the Olympic rings, which made them the most-recognised symbol. They were followed by the McDonald's and Shell emblems (88%), Mercedes (74%) and the United Nations (36%).
>
> (SRI Sponsorship Research International, in IOC 2002c)

Yet, it is important to remember that the IOC and NOCs are constituted as not-for-profit organizations and all of the money generated by their revenue streams is re-distributed into the Olympic family, which includes the hosting of the Olympic Games, along with ongoing sport, cultural and educational activity in all countries served by an NOC.

INCOME GENERATION

The two primary reference points for the Olympic movement's financial interests are the IOC Marketing Fact File (2011) and the IOC Annual Final Reports (e.g. IOC 2008), which detail all sources of income for the IOC and how they are distributed throughout the Olympic family. Additionally, for in-depth analyses of the economic dimensions of the Olympics, Preuss (2006) provides an unparalleled depth of insight. The principal sources of revenue are defined within the IOC as 'marketing' streams which, as Toohey and Veal (2007) note, stem from the way the IOC perceives its relationship to commercial entities:

> The 'product' of the Olympic Games is provided free to the consumer. Revenue is generated not from selling the product to the consumers (Games spectators) but by selling the rights to use the product as a vehicle for marketing other products (products sold through television advertising and products sold by Olympic sponsors)
>
> (Toohey and Veal 2007: 57)

The five main sources of income for the Olympic movement are: (a) broadcasting right sales (television and internet), (b) the TOP sponsorship programme, (c) OCOG domestic sponsorship, (d) ticketing and (e) licensing. Over the period 2005-2008, the movement's total income was $5.45 billion, which excludes the income received by NOCs via their own commercial programmes. While all of this money is marshalled by the IOC, the organization retains approximately 10 per cent, while 90 per cent is distributed back to the movement (NOCs, IFs, and OCOGs). However, within these percentages there are important exceptions. For instance, exceptionally higher contributions are made to the United States Olympic Committee compared with other NOCs from both global sponsorship revenue (20 per cent) and USA broadcast revenue (12.75 per cent), a situation which reflects the large contributions made from both the USA television provider, NBCUniversal, and the fact that many of the TOP sponsors are based in the USA.[3] Moreover, each of the existing revenue streams is distributed differently for the three principal beneficiaries. For example, the money raised from TOP sponsors is divided into two halves, with 50 per cent going to Summer and Winter OCOGs and the other 50 per cent being shared in different proportions by the NOCs, IFs and the IOC. Additionally, the NOCs oversee and are primary beneficiaries of their own domestic sponsorship programmes, except when the Games are hosted in their country, whereby further distribution takes place towards other elements of the Olympic family.

Based on the latest assessment by the IOC (2010e), the breakdown of income streams for the Olympic movement is as follows: broadcasting rights 50 per cent, sponsorship 40 per cent, ticketing 8 per cent, licensing and other 2 per cent. The amount of money brought in through the sale of television rights has grown considerably since the first broadcast in the London 1948 Games when the BBC paid 1,000 guineas ($3,000) for the privilege. As a glimpse into how this has developed, here is a brief summary of the fees attributed to a number of Games: Rome 1960 – $1.2 million, Mexico City 1968 – $9.8 million, Munich 1972 – $17.8 million, Montreal 1976 – $34.9 million; Moscow 1980 – $88 million; Los Angeles 1984 – $286.9 million.[4] Since 1993, broadcast fees – as with sponsors – have been established in the form of quadrennia, which effectively commit Olympic marketing partners to two

Games editions (one winter, one summer). Beyond the fact that calculations are now made for two rather than one single edition, it is clear that broadcaster fee contributions continue to escalate, though Preuss (2006) notes that the inflation adjusted figures show a linear growth rather than the often assumed exponential growth. In any case, over two decades, the figures grew from $286.9 million in the 1984 Games edition to $1,494 million in Athens 2004 ($2,232 million over the 2001–4 quadrennium). Broadcasting revenue for the winter Games has also grown considerably, with Torino 2006 attracting $831 compared with $102.7 million for Sarajevo 1984 (IOC 2011b: 26). Reinforcing the desire to develop long-term partnerships within the IOC, the most recent broadcast contracts have been signed over six years from 2014–20, with NBCUniversal alone paying $4,380m (IOC 2011d), compared with $2,570 million from *all* broadcasters combined towards the 2005–8 quadrennium.[5]

The Olympic sponsorship programme is the other key marketing component for the IOC and currently represents approximately 40 per cent of total revenue (IOC 2011b). This programme is organized in three levels: the IOC world-wide programme or TOP (The Olympic Partners), the OCOG domestic (national) programme and the NOC national programmes (the latter of which do not contribute to the IOC financial reporting). Each sponsorship level offers the participant corporations the right to use the Olympic iconography in different marketing regions for fixed periods of time. While TOP sponsorship benefits the IOC and the Olympic family primarily, the main beneficiary of the Games domestic sponsorship is the OCOG (Brown 2000). As in the case of broadcasting, the volume of money secured by these contracts continues to rise. Yet, perhaps the more important point to note is that there are only a select number of companies who achieve TOP status and these are steadily becoming long-term partners of the Olympic movement. Beyond the eighty-year history of Coca-Cola, McDonalds has sponsored the Games since Montreal 1976, Omega since Atlanta 1996, and Visa since 1986. Indeed, even at the Athens 1896 Games, there was advertising in the programme by Kodak (Miller 1992: 45), a relationship that lasted until Beijing 2008.

Other sources of income for the Olympic movement are ticketing and licensing. Ticketing represents just 8 per cent of the total

Olympic movement revenue, but it is supposed to contribute around 20 per cent of an OCOG's operating budget. For London 2012, a target of £500m is set, which would offset a significant proportion of LOCOG's £2.15b operating budget. If it reaches this target, it would attain similar success to that of Atlanta 1996 and Sydney 2000 (IOC 2011b). Finally, the 'Licensing Programme' is also a key component of Olympic marketing and concerns the commercialization of products officially considered under licence by the host OCOG, NOC and IOC. Some examples of licensed merchandise include numismatic and philatelic programmes created by the IOC. It also includes the sale of Olympic pins, which is a cultural phenomenon at each Olympic Games and often a key way through which social interactions are fostered between fans.

PARALLEL INVESTMENTS: GOVERNMENT EXPENDITURE AND VALUE IN KIND

Each of the previous income streams provides money for the Olympic movement to invest in its infrastructure and programmes. Yet national governments also provide a substantial subsidy to NOCs on an ongoing basis, which further indicates how investment in the Olympics reaches far beyond what is typically reflected in the IOC or OCOG accounts. Indeed, beyond the IOC's formal revenue streams, there are ways in which the Olympic movement benefits considerably from other sources of investment, particularly those that are required to stage the Games. Most notable are the financial injections made by a host nation to stage the Games, which represent the single largest contribution of any Olympic stakeholder. Of course, these investments do not benefit the Olympic movement more broadly, and are instead direct investments to a specific Games and a city's future. For example, the British Government is projected to fund the London 2012 Olympic and Paralympic Games to a value of between £9 billion and £12 billion, with much of this investment going into London's physical infrastructures.

It is in these areas where disputes arise over how much the Games cost a nation. After all, the construction of an Olympic stadium may be a direct cost of the Games, but once the Games end, it is supposed to become an asset for the city. Equally, if there are city-wide improvements to transport and accommodation infrastructure, these may have been triggered by the Games, but they may also be seen as part of a broader regeneration investment that a city would have made anyway. In this sense, such investments should be reported as costs only partially attributable to the Games. Of course, not all Games require such an injection of additional funds and Preuss (2007) distinguishes between cheap and expensive Games. For example, the Los Angeles 1984 and Atlanta 1996 Games did not involve much additional construction of venues, relying instead on what existed already, while the Games of Sydney 2000, Athens 2004, Beijing 2008 and London 2012 led to considerable infrastructural investments from government. As we will discuss in Chapter 8, ongoing discussions on Games economics consider whether special infra-structural investments prove to be truly beneficial for the host city in the medium to long term or whether they are likely to become an additional burden or 'white elephant', not responding to real needs or long-term planning beyond the Games' immediate requirements.

Additionally, a crucial, but often overlooked, source of income for the Olympic movement is the value-in-kind funding that it receives from sponsors and providers on top of their cash con-tributions. Beyond the essential requirements of staging sport com-petitions, all kinds of organizations in the public sector may create allied Olympic programmes, which involve attributing part of their programme and operational budgets to Olympic related activity. This is particularly noticeable within the Olympic cultural programme or Cultural Olympiad, which traditionally has struggled to attract Olympic sponsorship and tends to be a secondary priority within the OCOG budget. The Cultural Olympiad thus builds instead on other existing budgets from organizations not necessarily accounted for within the official Olympic programme.[6] A good example of this has arisen within the context of London 2012, which has developed a programme of events called 'Inspired by London 2012', which works in parallel to projects funded by The Legacy Trust, an organization created to distribute public and lot-tery funds (£40 million in total) to 'act as a catalyst to link grass-roots activities across the UK into the Olympic programme, so that people from all walks of life – not just athletes and sports fans – can be a part of this once in a lifetime event' (Legacy Trust website).[7] Thus, if one were to map out the way in which the economics of a nation operates around an Olympic period, it would be possible to discern how funding decisions shift towards producing Olympic-related programmes which involve a tangible investment for Games-related activity, even if they are neither sources of new money that can be controlled by the Olympic family nor officially branded with the Olympic rings.

To conclude, identifying clear boundaries around what counts as Olympic economic investment is a challenge, requiring judgement over what kinds of costs are direct or indirect costs of the Games. Many such investments have an economic life that extends well beyond the Games. Equally, over the last twenty years, Olympic Games and mega-events more generally have become inextricable from the development strategies of city authorities and national governments. For instance, for London 2012, the east of London is undergoing a major transformation to accommodate the Games, which city planners insist will lead to wider legacies for the area ranging from green spaces, transport connections, leisure venues, commercial spaces and residential accommodation. In the Olympic Park itself, condominiums are expected to become highly sought-after properties and the EuroStar train will depart from the area, making the neighbourhood and wider region a hub for affluent, international business. To this end, it makes little sense to attribute these broader processes of regeneration wholly to the Olympic period, since similar changes would have occurred in some form anyway. Indeed, one may argue that part of the appeal for IOC members to vote for a particular place over another is evidence of broader processes of regeneration that are already underway and funded through the local city stakeholders. At the same time, as argued earlier, there is evidence to suggest that hosting the Games helps accelerate these agendas by building stakeholder consensus.

Regardless of how the costs are broken down, the economic financing of the Games is one of the most controversial debates that surrounds the Olympics and this is partly due to the apparent contradictions it embodies. Very often, the Olympic transaction takes place between communities which are less affluent, making way for those who are extremely affluent. This is exemplified by processes of urban gentrification, which often involve improving living conditions in urban areas, but at the expense of evicting existing communities. However, it would be unreasonable to claim that the Olympic movement has brought about this present era of hyper-commercial, multi-billion Olympic industry single-handedly, or even that the drive towards elite-led city regeneration is a uniquely Olympic phenomenon. After all, the catalyst for the renegotiation of broadcast and sponsorship contracts was the Montreal 1976 financial disaster, after which nearly no cities were willing to stage the Games. For the 1984 Olympics, only Los Angeles had been willing to bid for the Games and staging them required some creative thought over how they would be funded, leading to the first exclusively, privately funded Games. It was their example that inspired the IOC to reassess its funding structure and establish the 'New Sources of Finance Commission' headed by Guirandou-N'Daiye and subsequently Dick Pound (Miller 1992: 45).

The transformations brought about by this period of turmoil and uncertainty allowed the Olympic movement to invest in programmes that are not able to generate sponsorship, as evidenced by the large growth in Olympic Solidarity support. As Whitson (1998) points out, today's Olympic movement has made tangible commitments to Olympic nations and 'the revenue from commercial sponsorships ... has allowed the IOC to contribute to sport development in the developing countries and to subsidize their participation in the Games themselves, something that many new nations have seen as an important symbol of nationhood' (p. 3). Like many other forms of cultural enterprise, in an era of limited public funding, private sponsorship has so far proved to be the only way to fund such pursuits as the Olympics and the IOC's present model has allowed it to enjoy a period of financial stability the likes of which it has never seen before. Equally, the IOC's requirement of public subsidy for the Games can be seen as an attempt to avoid too much private ownership of the Games.

Nevertheless, in closing it is useful to remember that Coubertin envisaged that the value of the Games would only be realized if they remained protected from commercial exploitation:

> We have not worked, my friends and I, to give you back the Olympic Games that you could turn them into a museum piece or cinematographic play, nor to have them exploited by commercial or electoral interests.

> (Coubertin, cited in DaCosta 2002: 108)

In this sense, perhaps there will come a point when it will be necessary to restrict the Olympic movement's economic growth by introducing certain measures. For example, given the monopoly over Olympic symbol or brand associations held by TOP sponsors for whom the relationship has lasted decades, there may be a need to introduce a length of term in the same way that a length of term now exists for the IOC President. While this would make the IOC's task much harder, it might also contribute to a more rounded Olympic programme, where a diversity of interests would be able to organize their work around the values of Olympism. Alternatively, as we discuss in the next chapter, the escalating costs required to win the broadcast rights for the Games may effectively remove public service broadcasting from the Olympic programme, bringing into question the IOC's ability to ensure that the Games maintain their obligation to reach out to as wide a public audience as possible.

MEDIA AND COMMUNICATION

A defining feature of the modern Olympic movement has been its relationship with the media, particularly television broadcasters, which have been involved with the Olympics since Berlin 1936. As noted in the previous chapter, the prominence of the media in the IOC's economic infrastructure places each partner in a very powerful position. On the one hand, the funds derived from the Olympic Games broadcast contracts provide the Olympic movement with a stable and growing income stream. Alternatively, broadcasters are able to capitalize on their purchase and build their organizations through revenue generated by advertising. Nevertheless, despite this mutually beneficial arrangement, the agreements may compromise the integrity of the Olympic values and, as a result, the Olympic programme may have become the handmaiden of television broadcasters. Indeed, since the mid-1980s, there have been concerns that television schedules have influenced the athletics schedule, superseding the athletes' preferences or needs (Min 1987).

There have been various approaches to researching the media's role at the Games, yet there is consensus that the modern Olympics must be understood as a 'media event' (Dayan and Katz 1992). Dayan and Katz describe the Olympic Games as an example of the 'festive viewing of television' (p. 1) and go on to claim that the significance of the Olympics can be explained as a 'symbolic transposition of political conflict', which alludes to our earlier chapter on why the Games must be made sense of as a political project. In this sense, the media's role in reporting the Games is not just a matter of communicating sports events to the world, but is, as Moragas (1992: 17) describes, 'the promotion and selection of values developed through a complex communication production process – signs, rituals, images, *mise en scène*, advertising, information'. As such, the value of the media for the Olympics is not just in generating income. Rather, it is 'the principal cultural – and politic – responsibility of the Olympic Games staging process' (ibid.), a view borne out of the fact that most of the world's audience engages with the Games via the media. To this end, the Olympic Games may certainly be understood as spectacles, on Kellner's (2003) definition of how they 'embody contemporary society's basic values, serve to initiate individuals into its way of life, and dramatize its controversies and struggles, as well as its modes of conflict resolution' (p. 2). Yet, they also go beyond this and are complex cultural practices, composed of games, spectacle, rites, festival and myth-making (MacAloon 1987).

In this context, the present chapter articulates the breadth and complexity of the Olympic media, considering their role at the Games, while also arguing that change is afoot within the elite sports media industry. We begin by exploring how the media have evolved within the Olympics, considering some of the historical context to the present agreements between the media and the IOC. Subsequently, we explore the media structures at the Olympic Games and assess what kind of media work occurs around them, beyond the sports competitions. Finally, we consider what may be described as the Olympic digital revolution, defined by the rise of new and social media.

HISTORICAL CONTEXT

While most of the discussions about the Olympic media focus on the television broadcasters, they are just one form of media which operate at an Olympic Games. For instance, radio broadcasting remains a priority medium in countries where television is still a technology for the privileged, or where the broadcast infrastructure is still limited. Furthermore, while television is clearly the medium that dominates the average Olympic media consumer experience of the sports competitions, it may not be the most important medium in terms of contextual and non-sporting news reporting. After all, it is the printed news media that tend to exercise more critical scrutiny of the Games and the movement, whereas television tends to celebrate the Games (Moragas et al. 1995).[1] Equally, in the early decades of the modern Olympics, the printed press were the only media that covered the Games and, at the time, the concept of sports journalism was only just beginning. In fact, one may even argue that Pierre de Coubertin was the first Olympic journalist – a citizen journalist in today's terminology – as his extensive writings and high position in society allowed him to generate publicity through his own publications in newspapers and magazines.

Despite the importance of these other media forms, television has been the dominant medium at the Olympic Games for many years, in both financial and cultural terms. Funds from television rights fees constitute approximately 50 per cent of the Olympic movement's income. Indeed, for most people, the Olympics are conveyed entirely by what is reported on the television screen. While there are no precise figures on how many people watch the Olympic Games on television, official IOC sources claim that they range from around 2.4 billion to 4.7 billion people. Official viewing figures from the Beijing 2008 Olympic Games indicate that 61,700 hours of television were broadcast, reaching 4.3 billion people across 220 territories (63 per cent of the world's population) (IOC 2010c). The same source indicates that the most widely watched event of the Beijing Games was the opening ceremony, which reached 1.5 billion viewers. While some of these figures may require additional scientific scrutiny to clarify exact data capture methodologies, there is no denying that the Olympic Games attract vast television audiences and that no other event can claim such large figures on an ongoing basis (see Moragas et al. 1995).

Television footage on the Olympic Games dates back to the Berlin 1936 Games, with the first live broadcast taking place at the London 1948 Games (IOC 2011b). In these early years, the relationship between the IOC and television broadcasters was quite informal compared with today's exclusive, master contracts and billion dollar deals. Indeed, when the Olympic movement was just beginning, Coubertin was delighted that large networks would cover their own costs to come and document the Games at all. It was not until the London 1948 Games when the first exchange of money took place, which was a fee of £1,500 paid by the BBC (Moragas et al. 1995). However, challenges soon began to emerge in terms of how television covered the Games – either as a form of news or as entertainment. If television reporters were treated as news journalists, then this would require a degree of editorial independence that would otherwise not be afforded if, instead, they were covering the Olympics as part of their light-entertainment programming. In any case, it was the latter view which prevailed. This is not to say that the television news media are unable to cover newsworthy Olympic stories during the Games. Indeed, the IOC provides guidelines over 'Television News Access' for non-rights broadcasters which specifies the amount of television footage that may be used, along with restrictions of broadcasting around Olympic venues (IOC 2009e).

As global sports audiences grew, so too did the economic power of the sports industries and their capacity to generate advertising revenue. At the same time, competition for the Olympic television broadcasting contracts grew, arguably becoming a matter of pride for a broadcaster to win, outbidding their competitors. Indeed, towards the 1980s it became apparent that the Olympic Games was a route through which broadcasters could accumulate considerable economic value by having the privilege to transmit the Games. However, the Olympic family was receiving comparably little financial benefit from these arrangements. This did not pose too much of a problem until the IOC was nearing financial bankruptcy and required a new model of income generation to continue. These circumstances led to the development of exclusive broadcast rights contracts in the 1980s. As the financial base of the elite sports industry grew, it became clear that paying for the exclusive rights to broadcast the Olympic Games would translate into considerable advertising opportunities for broadcasters and this made a contract with the IOC very appealing and worth paying large amounts of money to secure.[2]

MEDIA OPERATIONS AT THE OLYMPIC GAMES

Ever since the financial restructuring of the Olympic movement in the 1980s, the media have become a powerful Olympic stakeholder and a key member of the Olympic family. The Olympic Charter specifies the IOC's commitment to protecting the media coverage of the Games, as well as the technical regulations imposed on journalists for this purpose (IOC 2010a). In particular, it identifies one of the goals of the IOC as being to maximize media coverage and for such coverage to 'promote the principles and values of Olympism' (ibid. 97). In so doing, the IOC asserts its authority on the media's governance at each Games. Moreover, the host city is bound by these requirements as an integral part of the host city contract. By extension, the IOC also asserts its exclusive rights by stipulating that,

> Only those persons accredited as media may act as journalists, reporters or in any other media capacity ... Under no circumstances, throughout the duration of the Olympic Games, may any athlete, coach, official, press attaché or any other accredited participant act as a journalist or in any other media capacity.
>
> (IOC 2010a: 97)

To secure full coverage of the diverse and concentrated range of Olympic activity during the sixteen days of competition, the host city is required to provide the media with state-of-the-art working venues, which are now commonly known as the Main Press Centre (for print) and the International Broadcasting Centre (for television), as well as Venue Media Centres within each of the sport competition venues. A fully equipped Media Village is also created to house journalists, providing meals and accommodation; media transport to Olympic venues is coordinated with the times of competition and an extensive network of information points is provided with the latest updates on all sports events and competitor backgrounds. Over the years, it has become apparent that establishing a centralized global broadcaster at the Games was necessary, the function of which would be to provide the international signal for all other broadcasters – having cameras from 200 broadcasters all seeking the same angles for covering the sports was neither practical nor desirable. After a period of experimenting with private tenders for contracts to provide this service, the IOC established the Olympic Broadcasting Services in 2001, which now transfers from Games to Games under the direction of the IOC, establishing a pool of personnel drawn from broadcasting organizations around the world:

> OBS eliminated the need to continually rebuild the Host Broadcast operation after each Games (new people, equipment). From Games to Games, the foundation would remain constant and it would be based on a methodology proven and tested from previous Games. A more efficient, streamlined and uniform Host Broadcast operation could be achieved.[3]

To control the number of media with access to such facilities, the IOC has a strict accreditation process following similar patterns to that established for the rest of the Olympic family (IOC 2010a). For press writers and photographers, the IOC has awarded around 5,600 places per Games since Sydney 2000. The accreditations are allocated per country, with priority given to the 'main media organizations' (IOC 2006a), which are determined by National Olympic Committees. As the driving force behind the growth of the Olympic movement, the television broadcasters are treated differently as the exclusive 'Olympic right-holders' with access to the core Olympic properties, such as the rings which can be used within their organization's brand identity. The rights are awarded on an exclusive basis per territory so that in any one country, there is only one approved official broadcaster and no competing TV channels can offer images of official Olympic events, beyond what may be fair use for news reporting. Broadcast organizations are allocated a set number of accreditations according to the level of funding support. In the period 2004 to 2008, the total number is approximately 14,400 individual accreditations to include presenters, producers as well as technical staff.

The two primary media facilities at the Games are the Main Press Centre and the International Broadcasting Centre, with the IBC being the more secure of the centres. They each share a series of characteristics, including a common process of accreditation and a Games time programme that generally provides information only about sports events. The non-sports dimensions of the Olympic programme – such as the Cultural Olympiad – do not typically have a significant presence at these media centres, or in the day-to-day programme of events taking place there. Non-rights-holding broadcasters may be entitled to apply for accreditation at the Main Press Centre to access and distribute text-based information about official events, but they cannot gain access to the International Broadcast Centre or the use of any moving images. This restriction extends to all press journalists. In addition to the formal media spaces constructed as part of the host city contract, the media also often operate out of other facilities. For example, NBCUniversal often has its own independent facility at the Olympic Summer Games, which can nearly rival in size the Main Press Centre. Moreover, the number of accreditations available to each broadcaster is often less than they would like, so media often book space around the city out of which it is possible to broadcast and set up their own studios on their own terms.

These accredited journalists receive access to Games venues and the exclusive right to report the official sports competitions. However, since the late 1990s, there has also been a growth in the numbers of non-accredited journalists who attend the Games and are interested in reporting non-sporting stories. In fact, at the Beijing 2008 Games, there were 11,000 non-accredited journalists, a figure which nearly matched the number of accredited media. As a result, the host city has created increasingly elaborate arrangements to accommodate the interests of this group at both Summer and Winter Games. These arrangements have taken the form of specially constructed enterprises, which have become known as Non-Accredited Media Centres (NAMC). These new media spaces still require an accreditation to access, but not one that is part of the official IOC or OCOG system. Instead, they are usually administered by the host city government agencies – typically the local council and its stakeholders – and the accreditations do not provide access to any of the protected IOC properties such as the sport competitions. Rather, these media centres are a gateway to stories that the host city government considers valuable to promote during the Games. The venue also functions as a government press office during the Olympics, staging daily briefings primarily for domestic journalists.

The emergence of non-accredited journalists highlights the challenges arising from shifts in traditional journalism since, in the absence of IOC rules or guidelines, the criteria for defining who can be a non-accredited journalist are much more flexible. In the context of the Olympics, these shifts have given rise to at least three categories of journalist. The most obvious is the accredited Olympic journalist, namely those to whom the relevant authorities have given certain rights to cover the Olympic sports (both print and broadcast). A second category is professional journalists who cannot obtain access to the sports, either because of accreditation limits or through not being rights holders. For example, if NBCUniversal sends more staff to the Games than its allocated number of accreditations, then its other journalists may operate out of the NAMC, rather than IBC. These journalists may also be at the Games to cover the non-sporting dimensions exclusively, perhaps for niche magazines – such as ski tourism magazines for Winter Games features.

However, there is a new, third category of Olympic media, comprising those journalists who are generally not professionally trained, but who have appropriated the identity of *citizen journalist* (Miah et al. 2008). This group has a more complicated relationship to mainstream media and encompasses reporters for blogs or specialist magazines. There are two further divisions within this category. First, there are citizen journalists whose work would be seen as a form of 'alternative media' who are opposed to dominant media narratives in society and dissatisfied with the contributions of the established Olympic media (Lenskyj 2000). These kinds of reporters tend to report content that aims to criticize the Olympic project and create disruption to the Olympic programme. The second category are those who are less ideologically opposed to the Games, but who *are* ideologically committed to everyone's right to act as a journalist and report on their direct experiences. In the case of the former, recent Olympic Games have shown how organized indie-media bodies can have an impact on the media ecology of the Games. For instance, Lenskyj (2002) reveals how there were two alternative media communities at the Sydney 2000 Games – the Sydney Alternative Media Centre and the Independent Media Centre, which each provided this disruptive function. Moreover, at the Vancouver 2010 Games there were anti-Olympic media communities in the form of the Vancouver Media Co-operative, which ran a series of protest campaigns leading up to the Games.

Alternatively, at the Torino 2006 Olympic Winter Games, citizen journalists from our second category were a strong presence at the Piemonte Media Centre – Torino's NAMC. Indeed, this was the first occasion in Olympic history when low-budget journalistic operations could broadcast in an effective manner through the Internet.[4] Torino 2006 demonstrated the challenge posed by such journalists to the Olympic movement, though this was not an explicitly ideological challenge to the value of the Olympics. Rather, it was a challenge brought about by the fact that these reporters had the capacity to publish high quality, multimedia content through diverse online platforms, leading to several infractions of the IOC's intellectual property. Since Torino, the network of Olympic citizen journalists who are not opposed to the Games per se, but who wish to report alternative stories about it, has quickly grown and maintained a presence at the Games. For example, at the Vancouver 2010 Games, two alternative media communities were created that resonated with our second category of citizen journalism. These were the W2 Center and the True North Media House, each of which was community based and utilized self-funded media participation around the Olympics as a vehicle for social mobility. Their work is documented in the feature-length film *With Glowing Hearts* (2011), which tracks the progress of Vancouverites whose lives were transformed by this experience. Ahead of the London 2012 Games, this network has developed into a UK and international community, operating under the name #media2012 (see Miah 2011).[5]

Together, the combination of an increased number of journalists who are not accredited to the main facilities and the emergence of new media suggests that the future population of Olympic media may be quite different from what it is today. Indeed, by the Rio 2016 Games, it is likely that the non-accredited journalist population will be larger than the accredited population, which in turn may change how the IOC and OCOG respond to their presence and Games-time reporting integration.

THE NEW MEDIA

Intimately connected to the rise of the citizen journalist and alternative media community is the development of digital technology. In the same way as it has affected all other dimensions of society, the rise of new media has quickly begun to have an impact on the Olympic movement. Since Beijing 2008, the IOC has created contracts for Internet broadcasting as distinct from television broadcasting, and it has formed a new commission on Television Rights and New Media to investigate the opportunities and challenges arising from this new medium. The impact on the broadcasting of Olympic content has already been significant:

> In four short years from Torino to Vancouver, we've witnessed the rapid growth of digital media. In fact, we now have the same amount of hours covered globally on the internet and mobile phones as we have on television.
> (Timo Lumme, Director of IOC Television and Marketing Services, IOC 2010c: 28)

However, despite our allusion to the way in which the digital revolution may unbalance the IOC's economic foundation, this explosion of digital content production has, so far, also reinforced the status quo, as those companies which win the television contracts are also the same ones which succeed in winning the Internet broadcast rights. To this end, the primary commercial asset of the Olympic digital revolution – the online broadcast rights – are still intimately connected to the same system of income generation that has operated for Olympic television broadcasting. Nevertheless, it is also important to acknowledge the cultural shift in how television is consumed, from being a leisure experience that tends to happen in one place within a private home – the living room – to now being a multi-screen, multi-location, 3D and often mobile experience. The implications of this are challenging for the IOC, as it may change various assumptions about how it delivers Olympic media experiences. For example, one could envisage the golden rule of the Olympia stadia – no sponsorship inside the competition space – being violated by mobile devices which are delivering content from sponsors via augmented reality whereby the spectator looks through the device's camera onto the playing field and sees additional content. In this situation, a spectator may also be looking directly at sponsor logos.

In one of the first articles published on the Olympics and the Internet, Toohey and Warning (1998) write that, in 1997, their search for 'Olympic Games' in the prominent search engine AltaVista returned 70,000 results. Today, a search for the same term returns results from anywhere between 15-40million on the search engine Google. Equally, the Atlanta 1996 Olympic Games received around 187 million hits to its website over the Games period (ibid.), a figure that was matched for *each day* of the Beijing 2008 Games (BOCOG 2008a). In addition to these statistics from official websites, Olympic activity exists on a variety of social media platforms like Twitter, Facebook and the photo-sharing website Flickr, the volume of which is very difficult to capture by web searching. However, as a platform with over 700 million users, social media networks like Facebook are now an integrated part of an OCOG's marketing campaign. Indeed, all three candidates for the 2018 Olympic Winter Games had links to Twitter and Facebook on their websites, with Annecy 2018 even mentioning it in their bid presentation as a sign of its strength. While this did not translate into a victory for Annecy, it remains clear that social media are becoming an important part of the Olympic movement today.

Since the Atlanta 1996 Olympics, the IOC has steadily adapted to the new era of webcasting and reporting in various ways. As noted above, it now broadcasts Olympic competitions live over the Internet and separate rights agreements exist for this. Also, in the last three years, it has developed relationships with the well-known video sharing website YouTube to broadcast Olympic sport to territories that do not have national networks. There are also signs that the IOC's approach to controlling Olympic media assets is shifting, recognizing that it may sometimes be advantegeous to permit the free sharing of Olympic media content, rather than attempting to restrict its use. In this regard, an important change occurred at the Vancouver 2010 Games, when the IOC co-hosted an event with the leading photo sharing platform Flickr (owned by Yahoo!), at which it broke with previous protocol by encouraging Olympic enthusiasts to take photographs at venues – even of athletes – and share their content online without fear of breach of intellectual property. Some months earlier the IOC also appointed a Head of Social Media and had already issued guidelines for blogging in advance of the Beijing 2007, Vancouver 2010 and London 2012 Games (see IOC 2011e).

There are a number of issues arising from this period that require careful consideration. First, does the rise of new media imply a different set of propositions about how the IOC ought to manage their media rights? Second, do new digital environments transform the landscape of journalism in a way that undermines the IOC's broadcaster contracts? Third, is the Olympic movement more or less effective in promoting its values in an era of democratized media practice? One of the key issues arising from the explosion of digital media content online is that it may transform or even compromise the role of the professional media at a Games. While the IOC continues to be concerned predominantly with protecting the rights of the moving image, it may become harder to protect this content or, indeed, the value of this content in itself may diminish over time, as new layers of content provide rich and distinct experiences. One of the emerging innovations in television is the integration of social media content, which could, in turn, transform the idea of a television channel as simply being the coverage of a broadcaster. Soon, viewers may be both watching a broadcaster's production and interacting with social media content at the same time. In the future, people will consume Olympic media content across different channels and devices, which may make older forms of media redundant. Thus, new media have the potential to expand the range of journalist communities that could be engaged around the Games and, owing to the vast number of people who, knowingly or not, act as citizen journalists and 'report' content from around the Olympic city, this may even overshadow the comparably small interventions delivered by official, rights-paying media organizations.

WHAT DO/CAN THE MEDIA REPORT?

One of the key questions that arises when considering the expansion of Olympic media via 'new media' is whether the new journalist communities are actually reporting anything radically different from an Olympic Games, compared to the traditional media. Thus, it is one thing to acknowledge that new media have changed who can be a journalist, but is there any evidence that this creates different kinds of journalism? This question is important when coming to terms with how the relationship between the IOC and its media is structured through exclusive contracts. While the IOC or OCOG cannot control the editorial freedom of the accredited Olympic media, the contracts held by broadcasters commit them to a number of broadcasting principles during the Games, which may be interpreted as a restriction of their editorial freedom. While the broadcasters' focus on entertainment is what drives the Games-time television coverage, there are interesting ways in which that is beginning to overlap with news reporting. For example, at the Beijing 2008 opening ceremony, the BBC anchor was the political news reader Huw Edwards, where usually one would expect it to be a sports commentator.[6] This may signal how the Olympics are becoming treated as more of a news event for broadcasters, rather than an entertaining spectacle. Yet, the more important way in which the IOC exerts pressure on the media is achieved by virtue of how the Olympic programme is structured. A sixteen-day programme of sports with events happening throughout the day and a limited number of journalists means that the work of the Olympic media is extremely well defined, leaving little room for in-depth reporting or the diversion of resources to capture breaking news, except for the host nation's media, which may have all their resources located within the host city. For foreign media, the Olympic Games is often the largest outside broadcast that a television company will undertake and it has invested considerable finances into promoting the celebration around which audiences will gather (BBC 2010). Individual journalists may spend nearly all of their time in the Olympic city located within a media centre, or based at a specific venue, rarely roaming out into the host city looking for stories.

One may make two interpretations of this set of circumstances. The first interpretation is that the Olympic journalist's experiences at the Games inherently restrict their freedom, since their movements are orchestrated to such a degree as to limit their ability to cover anything other than sports events. On this interpretation, there may be a conflict of interests where the ethical obligation to report what is in the broader public interest is given secondary importance to the prior legal contractual obligation between the media organization and the IOC. However, the credibility of this view may be compromised when further scrutinizing the media operations of an Olympic city. An alternative interpretation is that the IOC/OCOG have no ideological interest in restricting the reporting agendas of journalists, but the Olympic Games environment discourages the media from reporting those stories that may jeopardize their ongoing Olympic relationship. Moreover, to the extent that the personnel sent to report on the Olympic Games are primarily the sports journalists, then the decision about what kinds of narratives on the Games are newsworthy creates a natural bias towards only reporting the competitions themselves. When evaluating which of these two interpretations is most convincing, the relevant factor is revealed by examining what tends to get reported by the different media. However, what remains unambiguous is that (a) the accredited journalists are heavily managed by the Olympic organizations during Games time and (b) rarely is any story covered by broadcasters – particularly internationally – that appears to compromise the Olympic values.

A further distinction to make when situating the Olympic media is between the kinds of media productions that are created throughout the Olympiad, versus the Games fortnight. In this respect, the Olympic Games are clearly a catalyst for broadcasters to create new commissions that build audience awareness of the Games and provide a space for scrutinizing the Olympics in various ways. Thus, on the approach to an Olympic Games, it is common for television channels to programme content that draws on the social significance of this event. Sometimes this may take the form of documentaries about an athlete's journey towards Olympic competition. Alternatively, it can involve sophisticated pieces of investigative journalism. For example, during 2007, Channel 4 in the United Kingdom broadcast a number of programmes about China, to provide a political, social, cultural and economic context to the Games preparations and what they suggested about the country's global positioning. Similarly, BBC's flagship investigative journalism programme *Panorama* has produced documentaries about Olympic corruption, notably around the period of the bid for the London 2012 Olympic Games, where they endeavoured to expose malpractice in the bid process.

These examples of how media products about the Olympics enter the public domain are not all directly connected to the IOC relationships, but are to do with the broader programmatic goals of a broadcaster. Yet, collectively, all of these stories become part of the ongoing Olympic narrative, which is repeated every two years via the landmark of the Games themselves. During Games time, the ability of Olympic broadcasters to undertake more in-depth journalism diminishes and audiences instead rely solely on live sports feeds or pre-prepared packages about the Olympics which focus on the medal winners and so on. This restriction is what makes it so crucial to consider what kind of media population occupies an Olympic city during Games time. After all, who those journalists are, what they do, and how they are channelled through the Olympics world, has implications for what is represented and what the billions of people around the globe see and read. The imposition of the Olympic programme on the accredited media is why defining who is a journalist, what rights they have, and how they are served and managed at the Games is crucial, when considering what ought to be the role of the media at the Games. This is also why it is necessary to interrogate the notion of the Olympic journalist, which is gradually being transformed by so-called citizen journalists who want more from the Olympic media than just the sports competitions. This presents new challenges for the IOC, as the creation of new media centres and communities suggests.

MEDIA CHANGE

On the approach to the Beijing 2008 Olympic Games, the IOC took an unprecedented decision to broadcast the sports competitions to seventy-eight territories using the popular online video sharing platform YouTube. In so doing, it signalled how Olympic television *broadcasting* is changing, becoming more integrated with computer and mobile technology, quickly developing integration with social media providing personalized viewing experiences and being less reliant on professional broadcasters. At the same time, television *viewing culture* is changing, with less dependence on fixed schedules, a growth of multi-screen viewing and a diversification of channels. While the reaction from the IOC to new media is still quite recent, it is already apparent that new media have the capacity to transform dramatically the conditions of the Olympic movement today, not least because the experience of media participation online differs from media consumption offline. The collaborative, altruistic and sharing ethos of online media in a Web 2.0 era means that people are less willing to pay for services, especially if they are not optimized for social interactions. Thus, if the IOC's approach remains one of controlling information and communication, then the opportunities arising from new media may transform into threats.

However, if the use of new media involves a desire to transform the conditions of media participation, then it may allow the IOC to reconnect with its fans in ways that have not been possible to achieve before. It may also be a route through which the IOC can connect the philosophy of Olympism with broader philosophical approaches to improving society.

There are good reasons to assume that the Olympic movement will adapt to accommodate these changes. After all, since its modern inception, the Games have been a showcase for media innovation and this continues into the digital age. Over the last century, new forms of media production have emerged around the Olympic Games and sports generally, where the competitions have been a catalyst for innovation in such areas as slow-motion replay, under-water film capture, satellite broadcasting, high-definition, 3DTV, or mobile tracking devices to name a few. These developments reveal the intimate relationship between the Olympics and innovation, including their growing consumption via new media platforms.[7]

The present transformations in the Olympic media landscape may allow the Olympic movement to recapture a period when it was more closely aligned with Coubertin's ideas about its function as a social movement. These possibilities were made apparent in the case of Vancouver 2010, where media participation around the Games provided a mechanism through which people could articulate concerns about social injustices. Equally, the rise of social media means that NOCs can also make their work much more visible to their communities, since the means of media production are much more affordable and can be far more inclusive than was possible in a pre-Internet era. These possibilities suggest that the Olympic citizen journalists are now, more than ever, able to organize their media content professionally, producing rival productions to professional media companies. However, it is still unclear whether these circumstances will change – whether the IOC will seek to restrict such freedoms to report – given that they may jeopardize the economic foundation of the movement. Either way, it is useful to remember that the present arrangements for how the media pay for the Games and support the movement have only been around for a relatively short period of time.

Lenskyj argues that 'the issue of citizenship underlies all alternative media practices' (2002: 206) and the rise of citizen journalist practices in the Olympics and outside of it may indicate that media culture in society is shifting. Indeed, the alternative media centres at the Sydney 2000 Games advocated the view that 'Everyone is a witness. Everyone is a journalist' (from IMC website, cited in Lenskyj 2002: 166), assisting in promoting protests, allowing anyone to post stories to its website with 'no screening of materials' (ibid. 167). Yet, a media culture that is reliant on the free time given by citizen journalists, without any editorial direction, or institutional capital, provides no obvious route through which to fund the Games and this factor alone may determine its future at the Olympics. One final alternative for the Olympic movement's adaptation to the new media era may be for it to become its own media provider, including setting up its own television network. This idea has been mooted by a number of NOCs, most recently the USOC. While no such proposals have been taken forward, one may argue that the Olympic movement would have more control over its destiny and the ability to drive the values of Olympism if it had control over its own media. Indeed, in an era of new media, the IOC has begun to operate as a media organization and in key moments – such as the bid decision for a Games or the lighting ceremony in Olympia – its live online streaming is the primary media source for most of the world, since these are not events that broadcasters would typically dedicate resources to cover. Moreover, since 2009, it has created a distinct position within the IOC Communications structure dedicated to Social Media. The diverse platforms across which the IOC now operates, suggest that its Communications department is steadily transforming the IOC into a media provider, rather than just a body concerned with public relations.

In any case, it remains to be seen whether the IOC will dramatically revise its media relationships in the light of new opportunities to broadcast direct to Olympic fans. The IOC's media presence is already substantial through its social media identities and its extensive new, multimedia website, re-launched in 2010. It may only be a matter of time before the IOC decides to retain control of its intellectual property and broadcast direct to each country via the Internet, while negotiating its own revenue from advertisers. If this were to take place, then the next fifty years of Olympic Games reporting could be radically different.

LEGACY AND IMPACT

Over the last ten years, two words have shaped the strategic development, management structures and resource prioritization of Olympic host cities more than any others: impact and legacy. However, they are also words that are often conflated within debates about the effects of an Olympic Games. Here, we introduce these terms in very specific ways. We refer to impact as measurable, direct effects of the Games, such as the number of visitors that come to an Olympic city during the Olympic period. They are defined by reasonably tightly bound indicators, which can be measured either quantitatively or qualitatively with some reasonable assurance of connecting them to the Games period. In contrast, legacy refers to effects over a longer term, which may be difficult to identify in isolation since they may have been shaped by the Games as well as other related interventions over time. In the case of Olympic Games visitors, the legacy may include the feelings they have towards the city that persist in their impressions over a period of twenty years. For example, one may argue that the Barcelona 1992 Games created a legacy for the city that was about its transformation into a prime tourism destination many years after the event was over.

One may also discern differences between these two concepts by examining how they are used within Olympic discourse. For instance, within an IOC Media Fact Sheet used around the Vancouver 2010 Games, it refers to each in the following way:

> As the Olympic Games have grown to become the world's foremost sporting event, their impact on a host city and country has also increased. This has meant that cities interested in hosting the Games are now placing more and more emphasis on the legacies that such an event could leave for their citizens and, in many cases, they are using the Games principally as a catalyst for urban renewal.
>
> (IOC 2010d)

Here, impact may have to do with the immediate opportunities as well as risks that an Olympic Games presents for a city, be it possibilities for economic growth or potential environmental damage. In this context, legacy is referred to as having forethought about those possible risks, to ensure that what is left behind is something that has enriched a city, rather than become a burden. Moreover, strategic thought around the legacies of the Olympics is required to ensure that the impact is optimal rather than a negative consequence of the Games. In short, being able to 'promote a positive legacy' (IOC 2010a) from the Games implies having a good understanding of their impact and mitigating against any risks.

This chapter outlines some of the key issues facing the definition of legacy and impact evaluation targets within the Olympic Games, while raising questions about the meaning of each. We begin by offering some further historical context to the recent debates within the IOC about legacy and impact. Next, we focus on the development of discussion about legacy as a broad term and aspiration that encompasses urban and environmental as well as economic, social and cultural fields. Subsequently, we consider how impact assessments have been developed within the Olympic movement, examining the growing attention paid by respective local hosts as well as global partners to capturing Olympic impacts, and how this translates into a sophisticated international framework for research, evaluation and transfer of knowledge. Throughout this inquiry we discuss what kinds of legacy the Olympic Games leave for their host cities and whether they are sustainable. Furthermore, we consider what kind of evidence base exists to ensure that lessons are learned and shared from one Games to the next.

HISTORICAL CONTEXT

While discussions about legacy and impact have been central to event-hosting processes worldwide since the late 1980s, it was not until 2002 that the IOC introduced the notion of legacy for the first time in a formal capacity, at a conference hosted in Lausanne. In a message to the delegation, IOC President Jacques Rogge recognized that: 'It is very important for the IOC to be able to define the legacy of its main activity, the Olympic Games' (Rogge 2002b: 13). He went on to acknowledge that the Olympic Games 'bring with them a social responsibility to ensure that the organising cities have a positive legacy' (ibid.). As a consequence, the IOC outlined its explicit commitment to providing forethought on Olympic Games legacies, establishing rules and guidelines for the staging of sixteen days of world sport. It also committed to providing leadership to OCOGs on how to document what happens after the Games are over, in order to monitor the impact and promote positive legacies.

The reasons for such a recent emphasis on understanding the Games' aftermath derived from three main pressures on Olympic organizers at the time. First, in the wake of the IOC corruption crisis in 1999, there was a growing public expectation of greater transparency, accountability and demand for the Olympic family to take on responsibility about the effect of hosting the Games. Second, there was a growing awareness of the possible negative effects of hosting the Games for the host city, from large deficits to growing social inequalities which, throughout the 1990s, had led to ever more vocal campaigns of opposition to Games bids in countries such as Canada. Indeed, the most dramatic example of this was Montreal 1976. Finally, there were growing concerns that the Olympic Games had a damaging effect on the local environment where they were staged.

Since the 2002 conference, the word 'legacy' now appears throughout Olympic Games literature and is ubiquitous in the rhetoric surrounding host city plans. This recognition may be contrasted with the more common practices up to the late 1990s when legacy conversations would emerge only after the event. Today, they are a formal part of the bid process, where candidate cities are required to explain their legacy vision in the first chapter of their Candidature file.

In parallel with the growing discourse on Olympic *legacy*, debates about *impact* have become a focal point of publicly funded mega-projects in recent years. From such a diverse range of events as the European Capital of Culture, to the World Cup, the justification for public investment is based on the expectation of long-term positive impacts that may result from the experience. In the context of the Games, the IOC has committed itself to establishing a system to maximize the opportunities for sharing the lessons from every Olympic host experience through a transfer of knowledge programme known as Olympic Games Knowledge Management (IOC 2009a). In parallel to this, it has devised an ambitious longitudinal impact evaluation framework to monitor change across a wide selection of Games impact indicators, as discussed in the last section.

DEFINING OLYMPIC LEGACY

Today, legacy debates are a defining discourse within all aspects of the Olympic hosting experience, from considerations about environmental sustainability to debates about social inclusion, which have become core dimensions of responsible mega-event hosting. However, expectations about legacy vary and are often dependent on which communities or organizations are seeking the legacy. For instance, it is common for the Games to result in displaced communities, as new venues are created that require the appropriation of a range of urban spaces. Seven years ahead of Rio 2016, there has already been varied reporting of 'forced evictions', an issue that also attracted international headlines in the lead-up to Beijing 2008 and to varying degrees in London 2012. Yet, while the transformation of an urban environment may produce such negative short-term legacies, notably the destruction of communities that are relocated in order to make way for the Olympic venues, those in favour of the changes would argue that this process enables valuable long-term legacies, such as improved facilities, new housing or new business space to attract a previously non-existent workforce to the area.

A key component of the legacy debate has been the need to work towards *sustainable* legacies. This concept has its roots within discussions about environmental concern, but has expanded to encompass all dimensions of the mega-event hosting process. Thus, an Olympic stadium may be a valuable legacy of the Games in terms of it being an economic asset or a venue for sports activity, but without a sustainability strategy, this value may quickly be lost, as has been seen at various Games, most recently Athens 2004. Alternatively, the new skills and experiences developed as a result of a city hosting a Games, such as models of cooperation across public sector departments or the adoption of new working models with the private sector, require support systems to ensure they continue to flourish.

Moragas et al. (2002) identify six key Games legacies and group them as: (1) urban and environmental; (2) sporting; (3) economic and tourism related; (4) political; (5) cultural, social and communication related; and (6) educational. These are common Olympic legacy groupings within the literature and have also shaped OCOG priorities when developing strategic visions around legacy. For example, the London 2012 Candidature highlighted four key dimensions of their legacies naming them as sport, community, environment and economic, which, upon closer inspection, encompass the six parameters outlined by Moragas et al. (2002). However, even within the initial IOC legacy conference there was considerable disagreement about how these concepts should be understood within the Olympic context. A range of speakers noted that, beyond the most common categories of legacy – which tend to be tangible and measurable – it is also necessary to consider less tangible legacies, such as 'emotional' effects (Cashman 2002), which may involve the 'post-Games depression and even a sense of mourning for the loss of the Games' (p. 34). Several references were also made to the unforeseen or unplanned outcomes of hosting the Games, which may be either positive or negative (Cashman 2006, Preuss 2007). Indeed, this highlights one of the difficulties with the legacy rhetoric within the Olympic movement – particularly an OCOG – which often obscure the acknowledgement of negative legacies that emerge around the Games.

There are two primary challenges to the definition and identification of legacies. One has to do with approaches to measurement and the other about the difficulty finding a universal meaning. As indicated at the start, acknowledging certain legacies is limited in part by the difficulty researchers have had in measuring them, owing to their developing over a period of time and being influenced by a wide range of variables. This is even more difficult with so-called *intangible* legacies – such as the effect of the Olympics on national pride. Indeed, the challenge over measurement explains the secondary presence of intangible legacies within the kind of pragmatic and outcome-oriented reporting of Olympic host cities and stakeholders. Yet, the paradox is that, despite the difficulty in measuring them, these kinds of legacy (pride, image change, etc.) are also among the most prominent articulations of benefit within host city rhetoric (Jinxia and Mangan 2008). Of equal concern over how we define legacies is the fact that the meaning of the word differs across cultures and languages (for instance, in French or Spanish the meaning is closer to 'heritage' and takes a different set of connotations). Thus, MacAloon (2002) argues against a universal Olympic legacy structure that should apply to all Olympic family members.

A parallel definitional matter is about where the emphasis on promoting legacies should be located – legacies either for the host cities or the Olympic movement. As it stands, the legacy discourse is dominated by host city concerns, arising partly out of the IOC Olympic Games Study Commission (Pound 2003) which highlights the need to ensure that host cities manage the Games effectively and ensure reasonable expectations rather than allowing the Games hosting process to get unnecessarily ambitious and out of control. In this context, the Olympic legacy discourse tends to focus on three main dimensions: the effects of the Games on their urban environment, on the economy and on wider cultural and social practices.

URBAN AND ENVIRONMENTAL LEGACIES

The urban legacy of an Olympic Games is often a prominent feature of a host city's bid strategy, highlighting the event's potential to bring about the positive regeneration of an area. Roult and Lefebvre (2010) argue that 'to talk about Olympic Games nowadays does not simply mean an analysis of this phenomenon as a sport or an event, but to understand how, as considerable as it is, it assimilates globalized urban logics' (p. 2732). However, such authors as Andranovich et al. (2001) are sceptical, arguing that there are various dangers associated with basing urban regeneration strategies on the potential fortunes of a mega-event. For example, two of the most widely feared negative outcomes of the Olympic hosting process are the possibility of cities concluding their Games experience with considerable economic difficulties, or the possibility that facilities developed for the Games would become unused. The first has long been epitomized by the experience of Montreal 1976 (Roult and Lefebvre 2010), which recorded its last official payment of its C$1.5 billion debt for the Games thirty years later (CBC News 2006). The second concern is often referred to as the *white elephant* syndrome, which became a common phrase associated with Olympic Games host cities that were left with large, empty venues after the Games drew to a close (Mangan 2010). The promotion of urban legacy plans is also a response to the Olympic *gigantism* of the late twentieth century, which incrementally led to large and larger Games, involving increasing numbers of sports disciplines, event disciplines, more grandiose venues and growing numbers of accredited people. Equally, with the growth of debate around environmental concerns, notions of urban legacy have also been associated with the need to make the Games sustainable and ecologically friendly, which has involved scrutiny from world bodies such as the United Nations Environmental Programme or the World Wildlife Fund.[1]

Various authors have commented on how the Games have been used by governments as a catalyst for advancing urban redevelopment agendas (Essex and Chalkley 1998, Hiller 2006). For instance, Barcelona 1992 is commonly identified as a key exemplar of an urban success story, where the organizers made the city central to the Games design and the public experience. However, it is very difficult to prove whether the Games were the actual trigger or just a complement to these urban transformations (see Essex and Chalkley 1998), and claims over what happened and why they happened often become battles of discourses rather than of evidence. After all, within Barcelona, the 1992 Games may be seen as a complement to longer-term strategies of urban regeneration that were already taking place within the city. Alternatively, separating out the Olympic Games period from other socio-economic trajectories before, during or after the Games may be necessary in order to clearly evaluate legacy. For instance, how should one separate the recent history of the Greek economy from its having held the Athens 2004 Olympic Games? While critics have not discounted the importance of the Games as having been a factor in Greece's accumulated debt, it is questionable whether the Games are to blame in any broad sense. Yet, it is equally hard to deny that a more positive utilization of the physical legacies of the Athens 2004 Games may have altered its prospects, especially as 'Athens failed to realize its ambitions regarding utilization of Olympic venues' (Kissoudi 2010: 2793).

One may interpret the Olympic Games as a media event that has the ability to frame wider regeneration processes by placing key city stakeholders under the world's media spotlight. Indeed, one of the consequences of such scrutiny is that the Olympic Games function as a consensus builder, which has the ability to draw together otherwise diverse political views about the direction a city may take, so that various strategies can be pursued within a common time frame. In this context, both Olympic and non-Olympic infrastructural plans can be advanced and completed in record time. This has been the case for numerous city projects, such as new underground trainlines, which were completed for the Athens 2004 and Beijing 2008 Games, or the Vancouver 2010 SkyTrain 'Canada Line'. Alternatively, given the need to ensure a city is accessible to athletes with disabilities for the Paralympic Games, important social agendas around public mobility can be addressed around the Games period, which otherwise may never generate the level of public support to make such a difference to a city.

However, many of these positive interpretations of how an Olympic Games may affect an urban environment may equally be seen as divisive, in a similar way to how we discussed displaced communities earlier (as either the destruction of communities or the opportunity to rebuild places). In particular, there is often a tension between the pursuit of economic development and the pursuit of social justice, as economic growth within an urban environment often leads to the marginalization of certain populations. Examples of this include the development of the London 2012 Olympic Park, which is promoted by stakeholders as a great opportunity to improve the area's economic infrastructure, bringing in new investment, attracting a wider mix of residents, creating new jobs within previously non-existing commercial outlets, and attracting tourists to visit a new attractive park and attractive multi-use sport and entertainment venues. However, from a social point of view, critics argue that the development is excessively consumption oriented, insensitive to the small, historically rooted local community ecosystem, including small commerce and small production units which may go out of business.

Another criticism of Olympic Games-led urban regeneration is that priorities are often set in response to the ambitions of certain elite communities, rather than incorporating an understanding of diverse local community needs. These tensions have led some authors to question the foundation of the Olympic Games as a catalyst for any kind of positive urban legacy (Lenskyj 2002), and these concerns are particularly visible in the media from activist groups. For example, the 'Bread Not Circuses' community campaigned against the Toronto 1996 and Toronto 2008 bids on the basis of multiple concerns about the potential negative effects on the urban environment (CBC News 2001). Similarly, in advance of London 2012, a community named 'Games Monitor' was launched focused initially on exposing social concerns around London 2012, but more generally on providing a counterpoint to the Olympic 'boosterism' that pervades the discourse of key Olympic stakeholders.

The IOC's and host cities' recognition that positive urban legacies are not something that can be taken for granted led to the introduction of a new commitment within the Olympic Charter to take

> measures to promote a positive legacy from the Olympic Games to the host city and the host country, including a reasonable control of the size and cost of the Olympic Games, and encourage[ing] the Organizing Committees of the Olympic Games (OCOGs), public authorities in the host country and the persons or organizations belonging to the Olympic Movement to act accordingly.
>
> (Olympic Charter, Rule 2.13)

In the same year, the IOC also included a specific clause within its Olympic Games Study Commission report (Pound 2003) to warn against *gigantism*:

> The Games have reached a critical size, which may put their future success at risk if the size continues to increase. Steps must be undertaken and serious consideration given to manage future growth, while at

the same time preserve the attractiveness of the Games ... If unchecked, the current growth of the Games could discourage many cities from bidding to host the Games.

(Pound 2003: 10)

Since then, the IOC has discouraged OCOGs from creating larger Games, referring also to Coubertin's concern that

It would be very unfortunate, if the often exaggerated expenses incurred for the most recent Olympiads, a sizeable part of which represented the construction of permanent buildings, which were moreover unnecessary – temporary structures would fully suffice, and the only consequence is to then encourage use of these permanent buildings by increasing the number of occasions to draw in the crowds – it would be very unfortunate if these expenses were to deter (small) countries from putting themselves forward to host the Olympic Games in the future.

(Coubertin, cited in Pound 2003: 3)

Moreover, the IOC has limited the Olympic programme to ensure that no new additional sports or disciplines are added without the removal of another. As such, the era of excessive Olympic programming and infrastructure, typified by the Games of Beijing 2008, may be drawing to a close. In their place, the race for each subsequent Games to be the 'best ever'[2] may be less about the pursuit of excess and more about responsible planning. However, the growth in security and concerns about potential terrorist threats to host cities have also created an important new dimension to urban social legacies, such as the increased levels of surveillance that now take place.

ECONOMIC LEGACIES

A second prominent legacy debate concerns the economic dimensions of an Olympic Games. However, before considering the details of this, it is first necessary to emphasize again how economic *legacy* differs from economic *impact*, as these are the two areas most often confused or used interchangeably. When considering the economic *impact* of an Olympics, debates centre on a bounded period of time that surrounds the event, during which it is possible to make claims about direct or indirect economic investment and expenditure. For example, this may include how much money an Olympic tourist spends during a visit to the Games.[3] In contrast, an economic legacy concerns effects that go beyond this bounded period. In this sense, one may measure Olympic tourism impacts over the duration of an Olympic Games, versus Olympic tourism legacies over a period of ten years.

Traditionally, long-term tourism benefits have been among the strongest economic legacy expectations of Olympic Games organizers (Weed 2008). However, not all cities have benefited in equal measure from such a legacy. Some cities seem to have benefited from the global media exposure provided by the Games and strengthened their tourism base, such as Barcelona 1992 or Sydney 2000. For others, the Games have made little difference (Atlanta 1996), or have just experienced a peak growth effect for a very brief period of time, mainly in the build-up to the Games and immediately after, what Spilling (1998) has termed an 'intermezzo' legacy.

Other economic legacy claims relate to job creation. However, this kind of claim is often over-inflated or poorly defined. For instance, discussion on the type of jobs that emerge out of a Games hosting process often fails to acknowledge the fact that a large part of them are temporary or unskilled, mainly related to basic hospitality services and not easily transferable once the Games are over. Furthermore, the more specialized and high-level positions such as the chief executives of the OCOG and other leading Olympic organizations are often not retained within the host city. Instead, those individuals tend to become part of the cohort of transnational Olympic consultants that provide advice from Games to Games. In this context, it would be more appropriate to talk of immediate economic impact rather than sustainable economic legacy.

A more reasonable claim to make around economic legacies is that the Games can act as a catalyst or accelerator for inward investment (Essex and Chalkley 1998). Yet, the Games may be a high-risk route through which to create such legacies, given the amount of infrastructural investment that they often require. The Winter Games are considered to face even bigger challenges than the Summer Games to be cost effective. Preuss (2002) argues that the cost per capita is far greater, as the facilities required are complex, while the populations of typical winter hosts are small.

Overall, the area of Olympic economic legacies, while central to the discussion, justifications and aspirations of key stakeholders, is still a widely contested arena. There is growing evidence of direct and immediate (or short-term) economic impacts, but still a lack of clarity over how these translate into long-term legacies that can still be clearly associated with the Games, rather than other interventions. Of all the examples utilized to claim economic legacy, the reference to long-term tourism effects is one of the most frequently made and widely accepted. This links to another widely claimed and sought after area of legacy: that of image change or enhanced positioning for the host city. Yet, while image change is often presented as an aspiration that can result in tangible economic legacies (such as attracting tourists and inward investment), it is actually an *intangible* legacy, reliant on symbolic activity, such as effective communication strategies that lead to particular kinds of promotional materials and media coverage. Of course, if one can theorize changes in, say, the media reporting about a place and its impact on media consumers' behaviour, then this intangible legacy can be made tangible. In any case, the prominence of place-marketing in the context of the Games and the ongoing discussion by host stakeholders around achieving 'world city' status, as discussed in earlier chapters, are all part of these discussions and evidence of how it is not possible neatly to separate tangible from intangible legacies and how, in aspiring to understand any area of legacy, it does not make sense to prioritize economic imperatives without engaging as well with their wider social and cultural contexts.

SOCIAL, CULTURAL AND CREATIVE LEGACIES

Within legacy debates the social and cultural legacies are often treated as interrelated and, in some cases, there is good reason for this. For example, for the London 2012 Games, Arts Council England created a specific series of events called 'Unlimited', which formed part of the Cultural Olympiad. This investment promoted the creative work of deaf and disabled artists and one may argue that there is a social legacy that is advanced by this creative programme in promoting an awareness of the needs of people with disabilities within society. Yet, it may also be construed as a cultural legacy in the sense that it provides new investments in the artistic sector.[4] Another example of where the two overlap may be found in the volunteer programme. From a social perspective, one may argue that the volunteer programme creates new social configurations – perhaps dramatically increasing the volunteer community within a nation where it previously did not exist. However, culturally it also serves to create new communities and friendships which may last well beyond the end of the Games. In each of these examples, legacy may be interpreted positively, but social and cultural legacies may also have negative connotations. After all, the Games may have exacerbated social problems faced by a community or have reduced investment in particular spheres of cultural activity. Again, much like the economic and urban dimensions, separating out the legacies arising from the Games from broader socio-political process is a challenge. However, the central point is made most eloquently by Lenskyj (2002) when recognizing that, for the Sydney 2000 Games, 'there were strong indications that "Olympic legacy" benefits would accrue to the already privileged sectors of the population, while the disadvantaged would disproportionally bear the burden' (p. 131). Indeed, this reveals how the social and cultural are often intimately connected with the economic legacies. For instance, if a new Olympic park creates a dramatic rise in the value of land, then this will affect which populations are able to live there.

While such examples as London 2012's Unlimited programme or, indeed, the Cultural Olympiad more widely can have important social dimensions, it is important to distinguish the cultural legacy in terms of the awareness of and participation in creative practice, which may be heightened as a result of the investment. Alternatively, it may involve the creative exchanges that take place because of the connections built around the cultural programme of the Olympic Games. For instance, the London 2012 Games Cultural Olympiad plans a hand-over festival collaboration with Rio 2016 in September 2012 (Sharp 2011), which is one of many examples of how the Olympic Games foster new international collaborations.

Yet, it is also necessary to acknowledge that the notion of a cultural legacy is widely contested, meaning different things to different Olympic stakeholders. For example, MacAloon (2002) argues that 'culture is not just one aspect of Olympic legacy, it is the ultimate source of all other forms' (p. 271), because the Olympic Games contributes to 'increasing the accumulated cultural capital that will attract bids and hosts for future Games'. He also stresses the point that 'legacy – simply anything left behind – is not the same as heritage – that which is widely held to be significant in what is left behind' (ibid.). For the latter, sensitivity to the cultural and symbolic dimensions of the experience is paramount. Equally challenging is the fact that the potential sources for articulating a cultural legacy of a Games can be all encompassing. For instance, they may include the opportunities the Olympics bring for personal interactions between people or, more narrowly, refer to particular areas of activity such as opening and closing ceremonies, torch relay or Cultural Olympiad.

OTHER LEGACIES

Beyond these three primary categories of Olympic legacy, there are also areas that have had varying degrees of prominence across Olympic stakeholder legacy discourses. For instance, there is often discussion about the *educational* legacy of the Olympics, which coheres with one of Coubertin's key priorities for the Games. Indeed, OCOGs are expected to – and generally do – undertake extensive educational programmes around the Games period, though the legacy of these requires further investigation. Equally, recently, attention has been drawn to identifying the health legacy of the Olympic period (Dapeng et al. 2008). Closely allied to this is, perhaps, the legacy that is most often taken for granted, that is, a legacy for the sports community – both grassroots and elite. Indeed, there is an unequivocal prioritizing of sport legacies within Olympic literature. For instance, the IOC host city contract stipulates that any surplus money arising from the Games should be reinvested into the host nation's sports infrastructure.[5] Yet, it is also often true that investment in sports over the Games period becomes very controversial, as money is diverted away from grassroots sports to elite requirements, and as the pressure to win more medals for the host nation obscures other priorities to ensure widespread access to and engagement with sport.

DELIVERING LEGACIES

In accordance with event-hosting policies around the world, the pursuit of positive legacies has become a key commitment of

Games stakeholders, as noted within bid city documents and post-event evaluation reports. However, ten years on from the Lausanne 2002 conference, there remains a lack of clarity in the evidence base to support the claim that positive legacies dominate from hosting the Olympic Games. In part, this is because evaluations of a legacy may change over time and, indeed, may take some years to stabilize. The Sydney 2000 Games were among the first to fully embrace the legacy discourse, particularly within their post-Games assessment (Cashman 2006). In the immediate aftermath of the Games, there were anxieties about the legacy use of the Olympic park. However, ten years later, the Olympic park at Homebush Bay has become a popular site for events, suggesting that legacies may not be best judged in the initial period following the Games.

Yet, perhaps most disconcerting is the way in which legacy claims have become a core part of an OCOG's core justification for the Games. For instance, at the London 2012 bid presentation, the Olympic Minister Tessa Jowell used the word 'legacy' four times in her 300 word speech to IOC members. Moreover, London's CEO Sebastian Coe mentioned it in both his opening and closing speeches. Indeed, in all recent bids, the focus on legacy occupies the first chapter of bid submissions from candidate cities, highlighting its importance (see IOC 2009a). So great is this emphasis on legacy that one may argue there are unreasonable public expectations about what an Olympic Games can achieve for a city or host nation. For instance, each subsequent Games aspires to be the most environmentally friendly ever, or to bring about important social changes that require addressing. In so doing, there is both a culture of expectation for change, but also a relentless desire to have been better than all other previous Games. Nevertheless, even within an era of legacy-conscious OCOGs, criticisms continue to emerge in light of the poor immediate after-use of the Olympic park facilities. The Athens 2004 Olympic Games are perhaps the most recent example. Despite the best legacy intentions, the problem may be that, with an ever growing number of Olympic Games host cities, there remain still only a limited number of international events which can make good use of these large venues. In part, this is why the London 2012 Olympic Stadium has been created in such a way that it can be reduced in scale after the Games, to avoid a situation where a large stadium has no audience to fill it.

In order to keep a check of legacy promises and delivery, a wide range of organizations have been set up around recent Olympic Games with the explicit remit of focusing on legacy support or implementation. The most accomplished example of this arose around the Vancouver 2010 Games, in the form of the not-for-profit organization 'Legacies Now'.[6] This organization was constituted by the Province of British Columbia and the Vancouver 2010 Bid Corporation at the bid stage of the Games, to build public interest and, subsequently, to monitor the commitments made by the Olympic delivery authorities in the year 2000 – before the bid decision. Their early contribution to the debate aimed to prove that legacies are not something that occur after an event, but which begin with the bidding process. London 2012 has taken similar measures through the creation of the London 2012 Olympic Park Legacy Company, a not-for-profit public sector company, set up by the Mayor of London and British Government.[7] Moreover, the creation of the Legacy Trust by the UK National Lottery and public sector has enabled a fund dedicated to supporting the wider UK engagement with the Games, particularly around cultural activity. Their focus is to ensure that the Games lead to *sustainable* legacies in the range of areas we have discussed so far, but crucially these intend to connect with broader processes operating within the nation.[8]

In conclusion, the IOC has endeavoured to provide some degree of leadership by indicating a broad range of key legacy themes. All the same, the main strategic documents focusing on the Olympic legacy tend to prioritize the area of sustainability (green agenda). Undoubtedly, this is because the costs associated with large infra-structural venues can be substantial and demoralizing for a nation, as the Montreal 1976 stadium demonstrated. Indeed, they may leave the biggest burden for a host nation after the Olympics leave town. The models implemented by Vancouver and London for establishing independent companies whose job is to oversee the legacy targets may prove to be an appealing approach for future cities. After all, OCOGs are unable to monitor the legacy after the Games, since they cease to exist shortly afterwards. Equally, as noted, the most desirable legacies may not emerge until many years after the Games, so this requires a long-term commitment to assessment and benefit coordination.

KNOWLEDGE TRANSFER

The pressure to fully document the Games hosting process escalated in the aftermath of the IOC corruption scandal of 1999. The IOC Reform Commission report included explicit reference to the need for a 'Transfer of Knowledge' programme that could inform both the IOC and host city in more effectively protecting their investments (IOC 1999). This desire, along with the need for OCOGs to benefit from the guidance of previous host cities, contributed to the creation of the first formal Transfer of Knowledge exercise. Since then, this programme has developed rapidly and is currently established as the Olympic Games Knowledge Management (OGKM) programme, which is overseen by the IOC Olympic Games Department. OGKM activities have informed the parallel development of the ambitious Olympic Games Impact programme, which is analysed at the end of this chapter. However, first we provide some insights into key dimensions of the OGKM.

The IOC first implemented an OGKM programme at the Sydney 2000 Games. This initial pilot programme gathered data from just a selection of key functional OCOG programmes. The exercise had an important influence on the approach to collating Sydney's final report, a document that in past editions had not been held to the same degree of scrutiny and was often lacking in accurate and detailed information about key operations. Tests continued for Salt Lake 2002 and Athens 2004, with Torino 2006 becoming the first Games to implement a fully functional programme. Today's OGKM involves an extensive range of activity and documentation – both text and multimedia – dedicated to informing OCOGs and host cities. Notably, it presents information from the bidding phase, when candidate cities are invited to attend an introductory seminar. This may be particularly useful for the numerous cities to learn about the impact of their bid, which in turn may assist the city's wider strategic development. OGKM continues with bid city finalists and subsequent hosts being invited as part of the official observer programme during the Olympic Games fortnight. It also provides access to a 'network of experts with Games experience on a range of Olympic topics that the OCOGs are able to call upon throughout their lifecycle'. Materials gathered by respective host cities are stored and made accessible to future hosts via the IOC's online extranet (IOC 2006a). With the establishment of this programme, the IOC aims to provide key reference points for OCOGs and a standardized, evidence-based route through which to deliver Olympic programmes, particularly where challenges for delivery may exist. This is an important step forward given the traditional lack of detail of Final Games reports, which often read more like public relations exercises dedicated to highlight the Games successes, but without much useful information for those that were to host the Games subsequently.

Despite this progress in guiding the OCOG and taking greater responsibility over knowledge exchange to mitigate a host city's risk, there remain a number of questions about the merit of the OGKM programme in its present form, particularly its reliance on corporate frameworks to function as the ultimate source of expertise for the Olympic movement. The dominance of a small pool of global consultancy firms playing the role of key experts can be seen as a threat to more diverse local knowledge and expertise that operate around the Olympic movement. It may also lead to a failure to address local sensitivities, taking into account cultural values and the unique history that informs the character of any Olympic Games. Thus, this system of knowledge transfer also raises a question about the value of transferring lessons and information on issues that may be very site and culture specific. Nevertheless, the establishment of such a programme has eased OCOG operations and allowed greater dynamism by organizers, as they are now able to begin the hosting process with detailed know-how.

OLYMPIC GAMES IMPACT STUDIES

In parallel with the development of OGKM, the IOC has enabled the implementation of a transferable Olympic Games impact assessment framework, which begins at the bidding stage of the Games hosting process. This framework was originally called the Olympic Games Global Impact (OGGI) but was renamed the Olympic Games Impact (OGI) after it became apparent that proving global impacts would be beyond the scope of the study. Its scope was developed in collaboration with universities and international consultants involved in impact assessments and each instantiation of the OGI draws on similar partnerships as an IOC requirement. Its main focus has been to establish a fixed set of indicators spread across what are presented as the 'three internationally recognised areas of sustainable development: economic, socio-cultural, and environmental' (University of East London and the Thames Gateway Institute for Sustainability 2010: 6).

The identification of key impact indicators is a very new area of research inquiry and in the context of the Games, the methodology behind the study is revisited after each Games assessment. As such, it is difficult to be precise on what are the most appropriate methodologies through which to study impact, as these are essentially contested ideas. Indeed, the range of Olympic Games Impact indicators thus far has already changed over the years. Thus, in 2006, the IOC identified 160 indicators (IOC 2006c) while, by 2011, the teams implementing OGI in the context of London 2012 have proposed 120 indicators at most, of which 73 are mandatory and 47 optional (University of East London and the Thames Gateway Institute for Sustainability 2010). However, the IOC has emphasized the value of retaining the same core indicators in order to maximize opportunities for comparison and longitudinal monitoring.

Indicators are divided into 'context and event' which are explained by the University of East London OGI Report:

> An indicator is referred to as a context indicator if what it measures relates more to the environment in which the Games will be staged, the general context, a broader scale or is not directly related to the Games. An indicator is referred to as an event indicator if what it measures is directly related to the Games, or it is highly probable that the staging of the Games will have an impact upon what is to be measured by that indicator.
>
> (University of East London and the Thames Gateway
> Institute for Sustainability 2010: 6)

The implementation of the OGI is now established as a responsibility of the OCOG from its inception, with requirements outlined within the Candidature Acceptance Procedure (IOC 2011c) and followed, since 2007, by an OGI Technical Manual. Vancouver 2010 and London 2012 are the first Winter and Summer Games respectively to complete the study as part of the formal Games planning agreement with the IOC. The IOC defines the OGI study's main objectives as the improvement in an 'understanding of the overall Games' impact; to provide Organising Committees with a consistent methodology to capture the Games' effects; to help Applicant/Candidate Cities and future organisers identify the Games' potential benefits and burdens' (IOC 2003, p. 21). Moreover, they add that the main goal of setting up such a process is to 'provide the opportunity to learn and constitute a body of knowledge, forming part of the organisers' and host city's legacy' (ibid. 22). Recalling what we discussed earlier as Olympic Games' impacts being 'bounded' periods of Olympic legacies, the data collection process takes place over twelve years, from the bidding stage (what is normally termed a 'baseline' within impact studies) to three years after the Games have taken place. Furthermore, the IOC requires that results are presented via four main reports produced at regular intervals before, during and after the Games. Importantly, OGI findings are now an essential component of the Games Final Report (IOC 2003).

In most host cities so far, the OGI has been conducted in collaboration with universities and established research councils. In the UK, the Economics and Social Research Council contributed to the pre-Games data baseline via its Economic and Social Data Service, and was followed by a Universities coalition in subsequent reporting. The Universities group was particularly adamant that the chosen indicators were appropriate and feasible in the UK context and recommended some minor changes to the IOC, noting that some of the indicators required could be best covered via a parallel 'Meta-Evaluation' exercise, to be undertaken in addition to the OGI.

The UK has been particularly ambitious with its London 2012 evaluation programme, building on decades of significant critical engagement with the notion of evidence-led policy-making and assessment of large scale events (see García et al. 2010). As such, the Olympic Games hosting process is being closely observed from a range of perspectives and major efforts are taking place to coordinate data collection and analysis. In particular, the implementation of a Meta-Evaluation is a pioneering initiative within an Olympic hosting process and an indication of London 2012 hosts' commitment to establish a coherent overview of all evaluation exercises. The major challenge in this process is to ensure that the right balance is struck between city based evaluation, UK wide assessments and between the emphasis on economic, social, cultural and environmental domains. Furthermore, the organizers of the meta-evaluation expect to include insights from university-led critical research, dedicated to uncovering major issues that may indicate areas of negative impact. These findings may then be contrasted with government and key stakeholder led commissions, which are focused on capturing evidence of achievements and positive outcomes.

There are a number of ongoing issues in the development of comprehensive Olympic evaluation mechanisms that arise from one host to the next. These concern the scope of qualitative research as opposed to quantitative. The emphasis on quantitative indicators is reflective, not only of the OGI model, but also the preferred approach of most national policy bodies in countries such as the UK which, for pragmatic reasons, tends to favour narrow quantitative measures over more nuanced qualitative interpretations. This means that certain important aspects of the Games hosting process, particularly in the areas dominated by symbolic or cultural values leading to intangible legacies, are difficult to measure and are under-represented or altogether absent from the OGI exercise as well as related Games evaluations. This can lead to the mistaken conclusion that cultural and symbolic Games activities do not result in demonstrable impacts and legacies. In turn, this may lead decision-makers to make such activities less of a priority in the staging of an Olympic Games or its assessment. Susan Brownell (2006) discusses the implications of this oversight:

> We still lack a good scientific understanding of the Olympic Movement as a social movement capable of effecting social change. Pierre de Coubertin had a vision that still shapes the Olympic Movement today, but in this age of science people expect concrete proof that a vision is being carried out. Beijing will be the first host city to produce a full Olympic Games Global Impact (OGGI) report. This is an important step, but [OGGI] will not assess the cultural fields that might be most interesting for the Chinese Olympic Games. For example, it will not measure the effects on cultural heritage – such as the preservation of culture to enrich the Olympic cultural programme versus the destruction of historical sites for new construction, the growth of traditional

sports versus their replacement by Olympic sports, or the effect of the Olympic Games on traditional cultural beliefs.

(Brownell 2006: 53)

Such gaps are the subject of ongoing debate within scholarly research and tend to be at the heart of research priorities for established Olympic Studies Centres, as well as other independent academic researchers. Advancements in qualitative Olympic research and the growth in arguments about the possibility to demonstrate the impact of interventions without relying on numerical or statistical analysis exclusively are important to enrich the debate about what the Olympics can or cannot leave behind and should eventually inform the officially sanctioned programmes of evaluation and knowledge transfer.

To conclude, the analysis of legacies and impacts may be seen partly as an ideological or politicized framework, within which certain interests are elevated and assessed, while others are played down and overlooked. Indeed, while the Games are often pursued by city stakeholders on the basis of an economic 'growth agenda' (Andranovich et al. 2001: 127), critics have identified that this tends to be based on a narrowly conceived consumption-based development (ibid.) which may not benefit every host citizen or may, in fact, disrupt alternative community traditions and practices. Given the relative novelty of Olympic impact and legacy debates, it is crucial that they be subject to as wide a range of interests as possible, so as to ensure that they reflect the multiple and rich dimensions of the Olympic experience. This means complementing IOC-sanctioned studies with independent research, to ensure coherence and continuity of methods from one Games to the next, along with opportunities to raise difficult questions and challenge established models of assessment.

CONCLUSION
THE FUTURE

Over 100 years have passed since the beginning of the modern Olympic Games and after various periods of instability, they are today stronger than ever before. There are more nations recognized by the IOC, more male and female athletes, more sports events and, of course, more money flowing into the Olympic movement at such a rate as apparently to defy any global economic crises. Still, how should we regard Pierre de Coubertin's vision for Olympism today? Does the Olympic family still function as a social or humanitarian movement, or did it ever live up to this aspiration? Does the movement continue to invest in social causes and are those elements which Coubertin valued – such as culture and education – still prominent features of the Olympic programme in the twenty-first century? Do Olympic Games host nations or, indeed, NOCs pursue a programme of educational reform and, if so, is this driven by Coubertin's vision of Olympism? Alternatively, has the rise of the global sports industries and the substitution of Olympic educators by Olympic consultants left behind Coubertin's ideals, which have instead been transformed into units of income generation, gravitating around the Olympic symbol?

Perhaps some of the lofty aspirations for the Olympic movement are too much to expect, or, at least, one can observe how such aspirations of bid city leaders are often brought down to earth quickly by the challenge of ensuring that, at the very least, the Games take place on time, on budget and without any significant disasters. Indeed, recent Games have shown how ensuring that these pragmatic core objectives are achieved is no easy task. Of course, a lot has changed in the world over this last century and, were Coubertin around today, he might have sought to modify his aspirations for the Olympics, taking into account the current state of the world. After all, for many countries, educational systems are remarkably different from the period in which the Olympics were conceived, as is our understanding of the complex relationship between mind and body that defined Coubertin's notion of the perfect human.

This is not to say that the Olympic movement is wholly out of step with contemporary social, cultural and political matters. Neither is it to accept that the high emphasis placed on its economic stability defines the entirety of its work today. Such institutions as the International Olympic Academy in Greece and the work of National Olympic Academies, along with the vast numbers of grassroots sports community members, many of whom aspire to become Olympians, are powerful examples of how the Olympic movement is alive and well. Moreover, as a mega-event that has a demonstrable impact on all echelons of public life when it arrives in a nation, the Olympic Games can still be a moment for a nation to reflect on how its society is organized and what values it ought to protect, at least within the areas of sport, culture and education.

When a city wins the right to host the Games, conversations begin about such a wide range of issues as the amount of physical activity young people should experience in school, the strength of the country's creative economy, or the degree of awareness of and support for the needs of disabled people. Moreover, given the manner in which an Olympic Games becomes a high, cross-party political priority for a host nation, one may argue that it has a unique capacity to be a catalyst for changes that otherwise may be impossible to achieve. Of course, the wide range of interests that converge on an Olympic Games also makes the event very controversial, as some communities will be frustrated while others will thrive. In this respect, it would be easy to single out the Games as an inherently divisive entity. Yet, provoking debate and potential disagreement with specific interest groups is part of any mega-event hosting process, be it the Olympic Games or a European Capital of Culture. Furthermore, any large-scale urban intervention leading to noticeable change is likely to generate strong feelings, whether it is support or opposition. Naturally, the expectation in any democratic society is that such a process of negotiation should be open to consultation and that – in the case of the Olympics – the decision to host the event in the first place, and go ahead with related interventions, should require overwhelming support and clarity on who are the principle beneficiaries, as challenging as this may be to identify with foresight.

A crucial part of this discussion requires acknowledging that the global sports industries also shape the character of Olympic sport today. Moreover, their powerful role in bringing the Games to fruition has become inextricable from 'broader campaigns to reconstruct the citizens of actual places as global consumers, and to celebrate consumer identities' (Whitson 1998: 2). The modern Olympic movement has been an instrumental part of nurturing this culture of sports consumption. These broader processes within society make it hard to see how Coubertin's vision would fit within today's world, which is sceptical of globalization and yet locked into a global consumer-based society. At the very least, one should urge caution when relying solely on the rhetoric of Olympism to justify the pursuit of hosting a Games, though not because the philosophy lacks credibility. Rather, the challenge is that the sports industries that surround the Olympics may limit any meaningful realization of the goals of Olympism, owing to the emphasis on commercializing the 'great symbol'.

Despite the seeming contradiction between the Olympic brand and the symbol, it is clear that Olympic movement leaders still draw on Coubertin's vision, rather than strive to create their own – as might be said of either politicians or philosophers today. In this sense, Olympism is flourishing within the discourses of the IOC and NOCs. Indeed, as the IOC discovered in 2000 when conducting a global marketing survey, it is these aspects of the Olympics that give it a special significance within society. Of course, Coubertin's vision was not singular, rather it evolved with the Games over his lifetime. In this sense, it is also misleading to suggest that Olympism is a fixed philosophical framework, which requires a top-down interpretation. Rather, it is a fluid belief system and has the potential to adapt to new socio-political conditions. Indeed, one may read Olympic history as a perpetual negotiation of the ideals and their implementation by multiple nations with which some of the ideals may conflict.

Over the last century, the world of sport has also changed considerably, not so much as an industry, but as a professional community. In particular, the rise of sport science and its many allied specialities within physiology, nutrition, psychology and sociology means that today's Olympic Games are defined in part by the entourage of expertise that surrounds the Olympic athlete – each with a financial stake in the continuation of this way of conducting the business of sport. In this respect, the Olympics would be just another event within the sports calendar, were it not for the philosophy of Olympism. However, one may question the balance between the success of the sports industries versus the success of promoting the philosophy of Olympism. As Segrave argues:

> Many people today do not know that the Olympic movement is dedicated to universalist principles of peace, reconciliation, magnanimity and the betterment of the human lot; fewer still are aware of the philosophy of Olympism, what it purports, and the promise it holds; and even fewer know that arts festivals are routinely held in conjunction with the Olympic Games as the consummation of a broadranging educational ideal.
>
> (2000: 268)

It is difficult to judge whether this is a fair assessment of the situation. After all, it is likely that, today, more people know about the Olympic Games than in the early twentieth century, as television has brought the Games to billions of viewers worldwide who otherwise would know little about it. It is also difficult to claim that there was ever a period when 'many people' knew that the Olympic Games were the representation of a movement with a philosophical perspective committed to humanitarian goals. To this end, one may accept that Segrave is right in his claim but, equally, accept that there is greater public awareness about the Olympics and their related agendas today than was the case a hundred years ago, when only a very select, elite community would be involved in the conversation. This is partly because, when judging what matters in society by the beginning of the twenty-first century, it is now undeniable that media coverage and publicity play a critical role in determining how matters are discussed globally and the Olympic Games have become the global media event *par excellence.*

Certainly, the Games have become the main locus for Olympic activity and, in part, this is explicable by the way in which media exposure is organized around the Olympic movement – primarily through the appeal of sports to fans. We might be critical of how the media coverage of the Olympic movement is restricted by its contracts. Yet, it is also true to say that the activity undertaken by NOCs and Academies in schools and in civil society more broadly exceeds that of any other period in history. Today, there are over seventy National Olympic Academies, countless congresses dedicated to Olympic studies, documentaries made about Olympic history, and so on. These elements may not confirm that the title 'movement' or 'ideology' is warranted when trying to establish whether the aspirations of Olympism today are held by the average member of a population. However, the reason for this may have to do with the fact that this ideology has not been popularized as a broader political theory.

Even after a hundred years, it may still be too early to judge the value of the Olympic movement. After all, it is only in the last twenty years that the IOC has built relationships with the UN, the Council of Europe and other such bodies, which are gradually shaping its identity and values. These are important but fledgling relationships and they may yet transform the Olympic movement even further. Over a similar period, Olympic studies has enjoyed considerable growth as a subdiscipline that has made an increasingly diverse range of contributions across the intellectual sphere. Indeed, the Olympic Games are now a rich subject matter for developing interdisciplinary research, in terms of both consultancy opportunities and academic research.

When considering what comes next for the Olympics, there are clearly some areas of vulnerability that may arise in the near future. For example, it is unclear whether the growth of mega-event hosting opportunities is compatible with the finite number of cities that are able to stage such extravagant proceedings. Equally, there continues to be a major imbalance in the diversity of locations that have hosted the Games, raising questions about whether it is a genuinely global event. It is also important that the Olympic movement does not take for granted the value attached to the Olympic ideals. After all, although the Olympic Games is an event that still upholds some of its original amateur principles – such as no prize money for winners – its distinction over other sport events is becoming less clear. In the past decade, other mega-events have quickly adopted humanitarian programmes to complement their commercial activities and can thus lay claim to upholding universal ideas in similar ways as the Olympic movement has done for more than a century. Moreover, the mega-event has become an all encompassing entity within global society, whereby what distinguishes the Games from other events is no longer the quality of the sport or even the fact that it has an extensive cultural or educational programme. For example, the FIFA World Cup has grown into another example of a multi-dimensional global festival, with important urban cultural policy implications. This was demonstrated by the Germany 2006 World Cup, where the mass appeal of competitions inside the stadiums was complemented by equally appealing public gatherings outside these venues and throughout urban public spaces. In this context, if the Olympic Games is to retain any point of distinction over other worldwide events, the IOC must take on the challenge to expand opportunities for people to have more rounded first-hand Olympic experiences, which clearly highlight that the Games is more than just a sporting event, and has far broader cultural values and symbolism.

In closing, we have endeavoured to reveal how the cultural, political and social significance of the Olympics is found at the interface between the collective memory that emerges out of over 100 years of symbolic historical moments, the lived and localized experience of Games organizers, participants, spectators and host residents, and the global mediated experience of Games audiences worldwide. Without due consideration of each of these elements, an understanding of the Olympic experience will only ever be partial. This is not to equate the ways in which a Games may affect one community with another. After all, some people have their lives completely disrupted or even destroyed by such mega-events as the Olympics. Rather, it is to acknowledge that attaining the full picture of the worth of the Olympics can easily be misrepresented by focusing on only one of these dimensions. Thus, an Olympic experience ought not elevate the interests of the remote audience beyond that of the local inhabitants of an Olympic city, but neither should local politics neglect to consider the broader impact of the Games on the global community. Our overview and analysis of what we see as the key parameters of the Olympics is a crucial starting point to achieving this broad understanding, from which demands of the Games and movement may be made more adequately by bid cities, local communities, event organizers and the Olympic family.

NOTES

CHAPTER 1 NOTES

1 The Olympic Games were based in Olympia. The other Games were in Delphi, Isthmia and Nemea.

2 In 2009–12, it received $2.2m from Olympic Solidarity (Olympic Solidarity 2009).

3 However, this principle may soon be challenged in practice, as discussed in Chapter 7.

4 One of the most famous stories is of that of Pheidippides, an Athenian herald who ran the distance that is considered today as a marathon in order to announce the victory of Greece over Persia in the battle of Marathon. Pheidippides was celebrated in a wide range of songs and poems throughout ancient times, inspiring the English poet Robert Browning to write a well-known poem about him in 1879. There are doubts about whether this story is true or just a myth, but its survival over the centuries inspired the founder of the modern Games to create the marathon race as a key component of the Olympic sports programme.

5 The Paris 1900 Olympic Games took place alongside the Universal Exposition and the St Louis 1904 Games occurred as part of the World Fair.

6 This confusion is not helped by the fact that the logo of the Association of National Olympic Committees locates a different continent inside each of the rings (see ANOC website).

7 In the past, actual doves were used, but at the Seoul 1988 Games, they tragically flew into the Olympic cauldron flame and were killed, leading to

a change in policy. The Barcelona 1992 opening ceremony was the last time when real doves were used.

8 Importantly, tickets for this venue are administered by the OCOG and have been offered for free to local citizens, an important gesture in a climate where many locals are unable to secure tickets for events.

CHAPTER 2 NOTES

1 Tokyo was the city originally appointed to host the 1940 Games but the IOC withdraw its offer because of the outbreak of the Sino-Japanese war. Helsinki stepped in as a replacement host but also had to cancel because of the widespread Second World War situation.

2 The film was visible only to those in the stadium, preceding the beginning of the ceremony's global live coverage.

3 This title borrows from an edited volume by Price and Dayan (2008) which focuses on how the Beijing 2008 Olympic Games were owned politically by the People's Republic of China.

CHAPTER 3 NOTES

1 This has been accentuated given that the cultural chapter within candidature questionnaires has traditionally been the area where applicants are allowed greater freedoms and thus greater opportunities to distinguish themselves from others.

2 The level of detail of such guides is extensive, leaving little scope for misinterpretation. For example, within the Torino 2006 Media Guide for the opening ceremony, the symbolic meaning of each visual element is explained with reference to Torino's history and often key actors within the ceremony have some important connection to its past.

CHAPTER 4 NOTES

1 See the No Sochi 2014 Website at <http://www.nosochi2014.com>.

2 The achievements of Olympic Truce are difficult to prove. While the examples we provide did actually take place, it is doubtful that the Truce initiative per se was instrumental to their accomplishment. Indeed, the focus on cessation of conflict during the Games may be unrealistic, but more modest aspirations can nevertheless be important contributions to diplomacy.

3 Equally, it is hard to see how opening up media access could restrict content, so the impact of this IOC intervention may have been far greater than just allowing the reporting of Olympic sports.

4 In fact, two days after he had been asked this question, Rogge issued a further statement saying: 'Needless to say, I wholeheartedly condemn terrorists and their vile acts — it is the antithesis of everything the Olympic movement stands for' (Rogge, cited in Brennan 2011).

CHAPTER 5 NOTES

1 The reference to the environment as the third pillar is difficult to confirm. Some sources indicate that IOC President Juan Antonio Samaranch advanced the idea in 1986 (eg. Greenpeace 2000, UNEP 2009), though others indicate that it was adopted in 1994 (IOC 2009d).

2 The only difference between the two contracts in this clause is the addition of 'post-Olympic use of venues' within the London 2012 contract, which may suggest greater emphasis on these concerns.

CHAPTER 6 NOTES

1 For an overview of the organizations recognized by the IOC, see the IOC website: <http://www.olympic.org/content/the-ioc/governance/affiliate-organisations/all-recognised-organisations/>.

2 The 2005 versions of the technical manuals are the versions that guide the London 2012 management, because they were the versions available at the time of the bid decision.

3 In 2009, the IOC President noted that this situation required review and it was reported that the disaffection over the present arrangements with the United States Olympic Committee contributed to Chicago 2016 not winning the bid (Michaelis 2009).

4 For an inflation-adjusted assessment of how these figures have grown, see Preuss (2006).

5 Around 40 per cent of this amount came from the US television corporation NBCUniversal.

6 The IOC 2000 Reform Commission recommends that OCOGs should not try to deliver their own cultural events, but instead should look to established cultural organizations to assist (IOC 1999).

7 See <http://www.legacytrustuk.org> (last accessed 13 April 2011).

CHAPTER 7 NOTES

1 While it would be naïve to suggest that broadcasters relinquish their journalistic freedom by signing a contract with the IOC, it may be equally naïve to conclude that editorial priorities across the organization are not shaped at all by this relationship.

2 A comprehensive overview of the media rights negotiations is offered in Michael Payne's *Olympic Turnaround* (2006), which provides the insider's story of how the IOC developed its economic power base over the last thirty years to become the most lucrative sports brand in the world and one of the most recognized brands in the world economic market. Payne's insights also help us to understand the link between the television rights and the development of the Olympic sponsorship programme.

3 See <http://www.obs.es>.

4 For instance, the audio-visual file-share website, YouTube, came online around the end of 2005.

5 This name refers to a Twitter hashtag, which unifies the content reported by this community.

6 The opening ceremony is an event that is more suited to the skills of a sports commentator than a newsreader, even more so since it relies on a 'script' that is given to broadcasters in advance of the ceremony. The script highlights and explains the various symbolic elements of the ceremony.

7 Alternatively, digital technologies pervade other aspects of sports culture. For example, scanning technology used to develop bespoke sportswear such as swimsuits designed to go faster, or running shoes that are designed around an athlete's unique foot shape, form part of the strategy of athletes who are seeking to gain an edge over their competitors. These interventions also bring new aesthetic qualities to sports, as athletes become increasingly integrated with their technological apparatus.

CHAPTER 8 NOTES

1 For more details about this, see Chapter 5.

2 This phrase was used by late IOC President Juan Antonio Samaranch to describe Sydney 2000 as the 'Best Olympics Ever', an announcement that arguably instilled greater competitiveness among subsequent host nations.

3 While one may expect that people will be keen to visit the Olympic host city during Games time, others fear that the Games are also a reason to *dissuade* visitors from visiting a place, owing to fear of increased costs, overcrowding, and so on.

4 In this respect, the broader Games legacy is to address disability in a much wider sense, as the host city must make provisions for Paralympic athletes whose needs will require a large infrastructural upgrade to the city on the approach to the Games.

5 More precisely, if there is any surplus money resulting from the Games, the host city contract indicates that this should be divided as follows: 20 per cent to host NOC, 60 per cent to host country sport programmes, 20 per cent to IOC (IOC 2009 Contract, p. 23).

6 For more information, see <http://www.2010legaciesnow.com/>.

7 For more information, see <http://www.legacycompany.co.uk/>.

8 Rather like impact and legacy, the words 'sustainable' and 'legacy' are also often confused. Olympic stakeholder documentation often narrows the concept of sustainability to the environmental agenda, while legacy has a broader meaning and use.

BIBLIOGRAPHY

Adi, A. and Miah, A. (2011) 'Open Source Protest: Human Rights, Online Activism, and the Beijing 2008 Olympic Games', in S. Cottle and L. Lester (eds), *Transnational Protests and the Media*. Peter Lang, pp. 213–24.

Alkemeyer, T. and Richartz, A. (1993) 'The Olympic Games: From Ceremony to Show', *Olympika: The International Journal of Olympic Studies*, II:79–89.

American Academy of Pediatrics (2005) 'Policy Statement: Use of Performance-enhancing Substances', *Pediatrics* 115: 1103–6.

Andranovich, G., Burbank, M.J. and Heying, C.H. (2001) 'Olympic Cities: Lessons Learned from Mega-Event Politics', *Journal of Urban Affairs* 23(2): 113–31.

Atkinson, M. and Young, K. (2002) 'Terror Games: Media Treatment of Security Issues at the 2002 Winter Olympic Games', *Olympika: The International Journal of Olympic Studies* 11: 53–78.

Ban-Ki, Moon (2009) 'Secretary-General's Address to Olympic Congress in Copenhagen (SG/SM/12514)', *United Nations*, 5 October. Available online: http://www.un.org/News/Press/docs/2009/sgsm12514.doc.htm (accessed 21 May 2011).

Barnard, S., Butler, K., Golding, P. and Maguire, J. (2006) '"Making the News": The Athens Olympics 2004 and Competing Ideologies?', *Olympika: The International Journal of Olympic Studies* 15: 35–56.

Barney, R.K. (1992) 'This Great Symbol: Tricks of History', *Olympic Review* No. 301, Nov. 1992.

Barney, R.K., Wamsley K. B. et al. (1999) *Global and Cultural Critique: Problematizing the Olympic Games*. Fourth International Symposium for Olympic Research, London, Ontario, The University of Western Ontario.

Barney, R.K., Wenn, S.R. and Martyn, S.G. (2002) *Selling the Five Rings: The International Olympic Committee and the Rise of Olympic Commercialism*, Salt Lake City, UT: University of Utah Press.

Berkaak, O.A. (1999) 'In the Heart of the Volcano: The Olympic Games as Mega Drama', in A.M. Klausen (ed.) *Olympic Games as Performance and Public Event: The Case of the XVII Winter Olympic Games in Norway*. New York: Berghahn Books, 49–75.

Black, D.R. and S. Bezanson (2004) 'The Olympic Games, Human Rights and Democratisation: Lessons from Seoul and Implications for Beijing', *Third World Quarterly* 25(7): 1245–61.

Blackshaw, I. (2003) 'The Court of Arbitration for Sport: An International Forum for Settling Disputes Effectively Within the Family of Sport', *Entertainment Law* 2 (2):61–83.

BOCOG (2008a) *Official Website of the Beijing Games Gets Almost 200 Million Hits on August 14*. Available online: http://en.beijing2008.cn/bocog/ bocognews/headlines/n214545765.shtml (accessed 21 May 2011).

——(2008b) *Bid Documents and Analysis: Passion Behind the Bid. In Official Report of the Beijing 2008 Olympic Games*, vol. 1. Beijing: Beijing Organizing Committee for the Olympic Games.

Brennan, C. (2011, May 5) 'IOC's Rogge Says Right Thing, Eventually, about Bin Laden', *USA Today*. Available online: http://www.usatoday. com/sports/columnist/brennan/2011-05-05-jacques-rogge-on-bin-laden_N .htm (accessed 21 May 2011).

Bridges, B. (2008) 'The Seoul Olympics: Economic Miracle Meets the World', *The International Journal of the History of Sport* 25(14), 1939–195.

Briggs, R., McCarthy, H., and Zorbas, A. (2004) *16 Days: The Role of the Olympic Truce in the Toolkit for Peace*. London: International Olympic Truce Centre.

British Broadcasting Corporation Trust (2010, 13 January) 'The BBC's Management of its Coverage of Major Sporting and Music Events', *Review by the Comptroller and Auditor General presented to the BBC Trust's Finance and Compliance Committee*. Available online: http://www.bbc.co.uk/bbctrust/ assets/files/pdf/review_report_research/vfm/major_events.txt (accessed 21 May 2011).

Brown, G. (2000) 'Emerging Issues in Olympic Sponsorship: Implications for Host Cities', *Sport Management* 3(1): 71–92.

Brownell, S. (2006) 'The Beijing Effect', *Olympic Review*. 52–5.

Burbank, M.J., Andranowich, G.D. and Heying, C.H. (2001) *Olympic Dreams: The Impact of Mega-Events on Local Politics*. Boulder: Lynne Rienner Publishers.

Campbell, D. (2006) 'BBC at War over "Mad" Olympic Start Times', *The Observer*. Available online: http://www.guardian.co.uk/uk/2006/jul/16/ bbc.media (accessed 23 July 2011).

Cantelon, H., and Letters, M. (2000) 'The Making of the IOC Environmental Policy as the Third Dimension of the Olympic Movement', *International Review for the Sociology of Sport*, 35(3): 294–308.

Cashman, R. (2002) 'What is "Olympic Legacy"?', in M. Moragas, C. Kennett and N. Puig (eds) *The Legacy of the Olympic Games 1984–2000*, Lausanne: IOC, pp. 31–42.

——(2006) *The Bitter-Sweet Awakening: the Legacy of the Sydney 2000 Olympic Games*. Sydney: Walla Walla Press and Australian Centre for Olympic Studies.?

Cashman, R. and Hughes, A. (1999) *Staging the Olympics: The Event and its Impact*. Sydney: UNSW Press.

CBC News (2001) 'Bread Not Circuses Voices Concerns to IOC', *CBC News*. Available online: http://www.cbc.ca/news/story/2001/03/09/tor_breadno tcircuses030901.html (accessed 17 July 2011).

CBC News (2006) 'Quebec's Big Owe Stadium Debt is Over', *CBC News*. Available online: http://www.cbc.ca/news/canada/montreal/story/2006/12/19/qc-olympicstadium.html (accessed 23 July 2011).

Cha, V.D. (2010) 'Politics and the Olympic Transaction: Measuring China's Accomplishments', *The International Journal of the History of Sport*, 27(14–15): 2359–79.

Chalkley, B. and Essex, S. (1999) 'Urban Development through Hosting International Events: A History of the Olympic Games', *Planning Perspectives* 14(4): 369–394.

Chappelet, J.-L. (2002) 'The Legacy of the Winter Olympic Games: An Overview', in M. Moragas, C. Kennett and N. Puig (eds) *The Legacy of the Olympic Games 1984–2000*. Lausanne: IOC, pp. 54–66.

——(2010) 'Third Pillar of Olympism', email (October 2010).

Chappelet, J.-L., and Bayley, E. (2005) *Strategic and Performance Management of Olympic Sport Organisations*. Champaign, IL: Human Kinetics.

Chappelet, J.-L., and Kubler-Mabbott, B. (2008) *The International Olympic Committee and the Olympic System: The Governance of World Sport*. Abingdon and New York: Routledge.

Collins, S. (2007) 'Samurai Politics: Japanese Cultural Identity in Global Sport: The Olympic Games as a Representational Strategy', *International Journal of the History of Sport* 24(3): 357–74.

DaCosta, L.P. (2002) *Olympic Studies: Current Intellectual Crossroads*. Rio de Janeiro: University Gama Filho.

Dapeng et al. (2008) *The Health Legacy of the 2008 Beijing Olympic Games: Successes and Recommendations*. World Health Organization.

Dayan, D. and Katz, E. (1992) *Media Events*. Cambridge, MA: Harvard University Press.

Dyreson, M. (2010) 'Epilogue: Showcases for Global Aspirations: Meditations on the Histories of Olympic Games and World's Fairs', *The International Journal of the History of Sport* 27(16–18): 3037–44.

Elcombe, T. and Wenn, S. (2011) 'A Path to Peace: Thoughts on Olympic Revenue and the IOC/USOC Divide'. *SAIS Review* 31(1): 117–13.

Espy, R. (1979) *The Politics of the Olympic Games*. Berkeley: University of California Press.

Essex, S. and B. Chalkley (1998) 'Olympic Games: Catalyst of Urban Change', *Leisure Studies* 17: 187–206.

Farrow, R. and Farrow, M. (2007) 'The "Genocide Olympics"', *The Wall Street Journal*. Available online: http://www.miafarrow.org/ed_032807.html (accessed 21 July 2011).

Florida, R. (2004) *The Rise of the Creative Class*. New York: Basic Books/Perseus.

Fussey, P. (2011) 'Surveillance and the Olympic Spectacle', in A. Richards, P. Fussey, and A. Silke (eds.) *Terrorism and the Olympics*. Abingdon and New York: Routledge, pp. 91–117.

García, B. (2001) 'Enhancing Sports Marketing through Cultural and Arts Programmes: Lessons from the Sydney 2000 Olympic Arts Festivals', *Sport Management Review* 4(2): 193–220.

——(2004) 'Urban Regeneration, Arts Programming and Major Events: Glasgow 1990, Sydney 2000 and Barcelona 2004', *International Journal of Cultural Policy* 10(1): 103–18.

——(2008) 'One Hundred Years of Cultural Programming within the Olympic Games (1912–2012): Origins, Evolution and Projections', *International Journal of Cultural Policy* 14(4): 361–76.

——(2010) 'Sydney 2000', in J.R. Gold and M.M. Gold (eds) *Olympic Cities: Urban Planning, City Agendas and the World's Games, 1896 to the Present*, 2nd edn. London: Routledge, pp. 287–314.

García, B., Cox, T. and Melville, R. (2010) *Creating an Impact: Liverpool's Experience as European Capital of Culture*. Liverpool: Impacts 08 – University of Liverpool.

García, B. and Miah, A. (2006) 'Ever-Decreasing Circles? The Profile of Culture at the Olympics', *Locum Destination Review*: 60–2.

Georgiadis, K. (2004) *Olympic Revival: The Revival of the Olympic Games in Modern Times*. Athens: Ekdotike Athens.

Georgiadis, K. and Syrigos, A. (eds) (2008) *Olympic Truce: Sport as a Platform for Peace*. Athens: The Olympic Truce Centre.

Gerlach, L.R. (2002) 'Church and Games', *Symposium: A Quarterly Journal in Modern Foreign Literatures* (August 1861): 13–28.

Gibson, O. (2011) 'London 2012 Olympics Countdown Clock Stops', *The Guardian*, 15 March. Available online: http://www.guardian.co.uk/sport/2011/mar/15/london-2012-olympics-clock-stops (accessed 1 September 2011).

Greenpeace (2000) *Greenpeace Olympic Environmental Guidelines: A Guide to Sustainable Events*. Available online: http://www.greenpeace.org/raw/content/eastasia/reports/guideline.pdf (accessed 21 May 2011).

Greenpeace (2006) *Eating Up the Amazon*. Amsterdam: Greenpeace.

Griseri, P. and Seppala, N. (2010) *Business Ethics & Corporate Social Responsibility*. Melbourne: CENGAGE.

Gunston, D. (1960) 'Leni Riefenstahl', *Film Quarterly* 14(1): 4–19.

Guttmann, A. (1978) *From Ritual to Record: The Nature of Modern Sports*. New York: Columbia University Press.

Halchin, L.E. (2004) *Athens Olympics 2004: U.S. Government Involvement in Security Preparations. (WikiLeaks Document Release CRS Report for Congress Received through the CRS Web, Order Code RL32497*. Available online: http://wikileaks.org/wiki/CRS-RL32497 (accessed 21 May 2011).

Hanna, M. (1999) *Reconciliation in Olympism: The Sydney 2000 Olympic Games and Australia's Indigenous People*. Sydney: Walla-Walla Press.

Hartmann, D. (1996) 'The Politics of Race and Sport: Resistance and Domination in the 1968 African American Olympic Protest Movement', *Ethnic and Racial Studies* 19(3): 548–66.

Harvey, R. and Abrahamson, A. (2002, Feb 07) '9/11 Flag Rises about the IOC Fray', *Los Angeles Times*. Available online: http://articles.latimes.com/2002/feb/07/news/mn-26739 (accessed 21 May 2011).

Hawkes, J. (2001) *The Fourth Pillar of Sustainability: Culture's Essential Role in Public Planning*. Melbourne: Humanities.com.

Henry, I., Radz, W., Rich, E., Shelton, C., Theodoraki, E. and White, A. (2004) *Women, Leadership and the Olympic Movement*. Loughborough: Institute of Sport and Leisure Policy, Loughborough University and the International Olympic Committee.

Henry, I.P. and Robinson, L. (2010) *Gender Equity and Leadership in Olympic Bodies: Women, Leadership and the Olympic Movement*. Lausanne: International Olympic Committee.

Hersh, P. (2011, May 2) 'Rogge's Refusal to Comment on Bin Laden Death Sadly Speaks Volumes about IOC'. *Chicago Tribune*. Available online: http://newsblogs.chicagotribune.com/sports_globetrotting/2011/05/ioc-presidents-refusal-to-comment-on-bin-laden-death-sadly-speaks-volumes-.html (accessed 24 July 2011).

Hiller, H. (2006) 'Post-event Outcomes and the Post-modern Turn: The Olympics and Urban Transformations', *European Sport Management Quarterly* 6(4): 317–32.

Hoberman, J.M. (1992) *Mortal Engines: The Science of Performance and the Dehumanization of Sport*. New York: The Free Press.

Hoberman, J. (1995) 'Toward a Theory of Olympic Internationalism', *Journal of Sport History* 22: 1–37.

Holmwood, L. (2008) 'BBC Facing Battle to Keep Rights to Olympic Games after IOC Snub', *Guardian*, 2 December. Available online: http://www.guardian.co.uk/media/2008/dec/02/bbc-sportsrights (accessed 21 May 2011).

Houlihan, B. (1999) *Dying to Win: Doping in Sport and the Development of Anti-Doping Policy*. Strasburg: Council of Europe Publishing.

Hudson, H. (1981) *Chariots of Fire*. Warner Bros.

Hughes, H.L. (1993) 'Olympic Tourism and Urban Regeneration', *Festival Management and Event Tourism*, 1: 157–162.

Hutcheon, S. (2008) 'Rejected: Ads Too Tough for Amnesty', *Sydney Morning Herald*. Available online: http://www.smh.com.au/news/off-the-field/rejected-ads-too-tough-for-amnesty/2008/08/07/1217702214139.html (accessed 30 June 2011).

IOC. (no date) *Olympic Movement's Agenda 21*. Lausanne: IOC. Available online: http://multimedia.olympic.org/pdf/en_report_300.pdf (accessed 21 May 2011).

——(1996) *Olympic Charter*. Lausanne: IOC. Available online: http://www.olympic.org/Documents/OSC/Ressources/Bibliotheque/Olympic_Charter/1996%20-%20Olympic%20Charter.pdf (accessed 21 May 2011).

——(1999) *Report by the IOC 2000 Commission to the 110th IOC Session*. Lausanne: IOC. Available online: http://www.olympic.org/Documents/Reports/EN/en_report_588.pdf (accessed 21 May 2011).

——(2002a) *Structure of the Olympic Movement*. Lausanne: IOC. Available online: http://www.olympic.org/Documents/Reports/EN/en_report_269.pdf (accessed 21 May 2011).

——(2002b) *IOC Crisis and Reform Chronology*. Lausanne: IOC. Available online: http://www.olympic.org/Documents/Reports/EN/en_report_590.pdf (accessed 21 May 2011).

——(2002c) *Opening Ceremony*. Lausanne: IOC Available online: http://www.olympic.org/Documents/Reports/EN/en_report_268.pdf (accessed 21 May 2011).

——(2003, Feb 20) *Candidature Acceptance Procedure: Games of the XXX Olympiad 2012*. Lausanne: IOC. Available Online: <http://www.olympic.org/Documents/Reports/EN/en_report_711.pdf (accessed 3 September 2011).

——(2005a) *Host City Contract: Games of the XXX Olympiad in 2012*. Lausanne: IOC. Available online: http://www.gamesmonitor.org.uk/files/Host%20City%20Contract.pdf (accessed 21 May 2011).

——(2005b) *Decision Containing Recommendations No. D/01/05, Ethics Commission*. Lausanne: IOC Available online: http://www.olympic.org/Documents/Reports/EN/en report_913.pdf (accessed 21 May 2011)

——(2005c) *Manual on Sport and the Environment*. Lausanne: IOC Available online: http://www.olympic.org/Documents/Reports/EN/en_report_963.pdf (accessed 21 May 2011).

——(2005d) *IOC Technical Manual on Communications*. Lausanne: IOC. Available online: http://www.gamesmonitor.org.uk/files/Technical_Manual_on_Communications.pdf (accessed 21 May 2011).

——(2005e) 'Legacies and Costs of the Olympic Games'. *Olympic Review*, (April), no pages. Available online: http://multimedia.olympic.org/pdf/en_report_928.pdf (accessed 21 May 2011).

————(2006a) *The Learning Games.* Lausanne: IOC. Available online: 2006b) *IOC Marketing Report – Torino 2006.* Lausanne: IOC. Available online: http://www. olympic.org/Documents/Reports/EN/en_report_1142.pdf (accessed 21 May 2011).

————(2006c) 'What is the Olympic Games Global Impact Study?', *Olympic Review* (June). Available online: http://multimedia.olympic.org/pdf/en_report_1077.pdf (accessed 21 May 2011).

————(2007) *Olympic Values Education Programme Toolkit.* Lausanne: IOC. Available online: http://www.olympic.org/Documents/OVEP_Toolkit/OVEP_Toolkit_en.pdf (accessed 21 May 2011).

————(2008) *The Olympic Movement in Society: IOC Report 2005-2008.* Lausanne: IOC. Available online: http://www.olympic.org/Documents/IOC_Interim_and_Final_Reports/2005-2008_IOC_Final_Report.pdf (accessed 21 May 2011).

————(2009a) *2018 Candidature Procedure and Questionnaire, XIII Olympic Winter Games.* Lausanne: IOC, Available online: http://www.olympic.org/Documents/Reports/EN/en_report_1451.pdf (accessed 21 May 2011).

————(2009b) *Olympic Truce Fact Sheet.* Lausanne: IOC Available online: http://www.olympic.org/Documents/Reference_documents_Factsheets/Olympic_Truce.pdf (accessed 21 May 2011).

————(2009c) *Code of Ethics.* Lausanne: IOC.

————(2009d) *Innovation and Inspiration Harnessing the Power of Sport for Change, 8th World Conference on Sport and the Environment.* Lausanne: IOC. Available online:

————(2009e) *Television News Access Rules Applicable to Non-Rights Holding Broadcast Organisations at the Vancouver 2010 Olympic Winter Games.* Lausanne: IOC. Available online: http://www.olympic.org/Documents/Games_Vancouver_2010/Internet_Guidelines_and_Press_Access_Rules/Television_News_Access_Rules_Vancouver.pdf

————(2010a) *Olympic Charter.* Lausanne: IOC. Available online: http://www.olympic.org/Documents/olympic_charter_en.pdf (accessed 21 May 2011).

————(2010b) *Final Report of the IOC Coordination Commission: Games of the XXIX Olympiad Beijing 2008.* Lausanne: IOC. Available online: http://www.olympic.org/Documents/Reports/EN/Br-Beijing-ENG-web.pdf (accessed 21 May 2011).

————(2010c) *IOC Marketing Report – Beijing 2008.* Lausanne: IOC Available online: http://www.olympic.org/Documents/Reports/EN/en_report_1428.pdf (accessed 21 May 2011).

————(2010d) *IOC Fact Sheet: Legacy.* Lausanne: IOC. Available online: http://www.olympic.org/Documents/Reference_documents_Factsheets/Legacy.pdf (accessed 21 May 2011).

————(2010e) *IOC Marketing Media Guide.* Lausanne: IOC. Available online: http://www.olympic.org/Documents/Reports/EN/IOC-MEDIAGUIDE-2010-EN.pdf (accessed 21 May 2011).

——(2011a) *IOC Activities, Highlights of the Week (13 May 2011)*. Lausanne: IOC. Available online: http://www.olympic.org/sport-for-all?articleid=128333 (accessed 21 May 2011).

——(2011b) *Olympic Marketing Fact File*. Lausanne: IOC. Available online: http://www.olympic.org/Documents/IOC_Marketing/OLYMPIC_ MARKETING_FACT_FILE_2011.pdf (accessed 21 May 2011).

——(2011c) *2020 Candidature Acceptance Procedure*. Lausanne: IOC. Available online: http://www.olympic.org/Documents/Host_city_elections/2020_CAP. pdf (accessed 21 May 2011).

——(2011d) *IOC Awards US Broadcast Rights for 2014, 2016, 2018 and 2020 Olympic Games to NBC Universal*. Lausanne: IOC. Available online: http://www.olympic.org/media?searchpageipp=10&searchpage=6&article- newsgroup=-1&articleid=130827 (accessed 21 May 2011).

——(2011e) *IOC Social Media, Blogging and Internet Guidelines for Participants and Other Accredited Persons at the London 2012 Olympic Games*. Lausanne: IOC. Available online: http://www.olympic.org/Documents/Games_London_ 2012/IOC_Social_Media_Blogging_and_Internet_Guidelines-London.pdf (accessed 21 May 2011).

Jennings, A. (1996) *The New Lords of the Rings: Olympic Corruption and How to Buy Gold Medals*. New York: Simon & Schuster.

Jennings, A. and Sambrook, C. (2000) *The Great Olympic Swindle: When the World Wanted its Games Back*. London: Simon and Schuster.

Jinxia, D. (2005) 'Women, Nationalism and the Beijing Olympics: Preparing for Glory', *The International Journal of the History of Sport* 22(4): 530–44.

Jinxia, D. (2010) 'The Beijing Games, National Identity and Modernization in China', *The International Journal of the History of Sport* 27(16-18): 2798–2820. Available online: http://www.tandfonline.com/doi/abs/10.1080/09523367. 2010.508275 (accessed 23 July 2011).

Jinxia, D. and Mangan, J.A. (2008) 'Beijing Olympics Legacies: Certain Intentions and Certain and Uncertain Outcomes', *The International Journal of the History of Sport* 25(14): 2019–40.

Kanin, D. B. (1980) 'The Olympic Boycott in Diplomatic Context', *Journal of Sports & Social Issues* 4(1): 1-24.

Kayser, B., Mauron, A. and Miah, A. (2007) 'Current Anti-doping Policy: A Critical Appraisal'. *BMC Medical Ethics* 8 (1): 1–10.

Kellner, D. (2003) *Media Spectacle*. London and New York: Routledge.

Kessel, A. (2011) 'Team GB Seek Olympic Stadium Dress Rehearsal at Student Event', *The Guardian*, 14 July. Available online: http://www.guardian.co.uk/ sport/2011/jul/14/olympic-stadium-charles-van-commenee (accessed 21 July 2011).

Kissoudi, P. (2010) 'Athens' Post-Olympic Aspirations and the Extent of their Realization', *The International Journal of the History of Sport* 27 (16–18): 2780–97.

Kruger, A. (1998) 'The Ministry of Popular Enlightenment and Propaganda and the Nazi Olympics of 1936', in R. Barney, K.B. Wamsley, S.G. Martyn and G.H. MacDonald (eds.) *Global and Cultural Critique: Problematizing the Olympic Games*. University of Western Ontario: Centre for Olympic Studies, pp. 33–48.

Kruger, A. and Murray, W. (eds.) (2003) *The Nazi Olympics: Sport, Politics and Appeasement in the 1930s*. Baltimore: University of Illinois Press.

Kwak, T.-H. and Joo, S.-H. (2002) 'The Korean Peace Process: Problems and Prospects after the Summit', *World Affairs*, 165(2): 79–90.

Lavaigne, A. (2010) *With Glowing Hearts*. Animal Mother Films.

Leapman, B. and Powell, R. (2008) 'Athletes Face Olympic Ban for Criticising China'. *The Telegraph*. Available online: http://www.telegraph.co.uk/news/uknews/1578202/Athletes-face-Olympic-ban-for-criticising-China.html (accessed 23 July 2011).

Lennartz, K. (1997) 'The Genesis of Legends', *Journal of Olympic History* 44: 8–11.

——(2001) 'The Story of the Rings', *Journal of Olympic History* 10 (December): 29–61.

Lenskyj, H. (2000) *Inside the Olympic Industry: Power, Politics and Activism*. Albany: State University of New York Press.

——(2002) *The Best Olympics Ever? Social Impacts of Sydney 2000*. Albany: State University of New York Press.

Loland, S. (1994) 'Pierre de Coubertin's Ideology of Olympism from the Perspective of the History of Ideas', in R.K. Barney, and K.V. Meier (eds.) *Critical Reflections on Olympic Ideology*. London, Ontario: University of Western Ontario, pp. 26–45.

London Olympic and Paralympic Games Act 2006. London: HMSO. Available online: http://www.legislation.gov.uk/ukpga/2006/12/contents [accessed 3 September 2011).

MacAloon, J. (1984) *Rite, Drama, Festival, Spectacle. Rehearsals towards a Theory of Cultural Performance*. Philadelphia: Institute for the Study of Human Issues.

——(1987) *This Great Symbol*. Chicago: University of Chicago Press.

——(1996) 'Olympic Ceremonies as a Setting for Intercultural Exchange', M. Moragas, J.J. MacAloon and M. Llinés (eds) *Olympic Ceremonies, Historical Continuity and Cultural Exchange*. Lausanne: IOC, pp. 29–44.

——(1987/2001) *This Great Symbol*. Chicago: University of Chicago Press.

——(2002) 'Cultural Legacy: The Olympic Games as "World Cultural Property"', in M. Moragas, C. Kennett and N. Puig (eds) *The Legacy of the Olympic Games 1984-2000*. Lausanne: IOC, pp. 271–8.

——(2011) Scandal and Governance: Inside and Outside the IOC 2000 Commission, Sport in Society, 14:03, 292–308.

Macdonald, K. (1999) *One Day in September*. Sony Pictures.

McGeoch, R. and Korporaal, G. (1994) *The Bid: How Australia Won the 2000 Games*. Victoria: William Heinemann Australia.

McIntire, M. (2009) 'National Status, the 1908 Olympic Games and the English Press', *Media History*, 15(3): 271–286.

Mackay, D. (2003) 'Olympic Committee Aims to Bar Wild Cards', *The Guardian*. Available online: http://www.guardian.co.uk/sport/2003/may/27/olympicgames.athletics# (accessed 19 July 2011).

McKay, M. and Plumb, C. (2001) 'Reaching Beyond the Gold. The Impact of the Olympic Games on Real Estate Markets', *Global Insights*, pp. 1–26.

McRoskey, S.R. (2010) 'Security and the Olympic Games: Making Rio an Example', *Yale Journal of International Affairs* 5(2): 91–105.

Maguire, J. (1999) *Global Sport: Identities, Societies, Civilizations*. Cambridge: Polity Press.

Maguire, J., Barnard, S., Butler, K. and Golding, P. (2008) 'Olympic Legacies in the IOC's "Celebrate Humanity" Campaign: Ancient or Modern?', *The International Journal of the History of Sport* 25(14): 2041–59.

Mallon, B. (2000) 'The Olympic Bribery Scandal', *Journal of Olympic History* 8 (2):11–27.

——(2006) *Historical Dictionary of the Olympic Movement*, 2nd edn. Toronto: The Scarecrow Press, Inc.

Mandell, R.D. (1971) *The Nazi Olympics*. Champaign, IL: University of Illinois Press.

Mangan, J.A. (2008) 'Prologue: Guarantees of Global Goodwill: Post-Olympic Legacies – Too Many Limping White Elephants?', *The International Journal of the History of Sport* 25(14): 1869–83.

Manheim, J.B. (1990) 'Rites of Passage: The 1988 Seoul Olympics as Public Diplomacy', *The Western Political Quarterly* 43(2): 279–95.

Maslova, N., (2010) *Green Olympics: Intentions and Reality*. Stockholm: Royal Institute of Technology. Available online: http://kth.diva-portal.org/smash/get/diva2:415837/FULLTEXT01>.

Mastrocola, P. (1995) 'The Lords of the Rings: The Role of Olympic Site Selection as a Weapon Against Human Rights Abuses: China's Bid for the 2000 Olympics', *Boston College Third World Law Journal* 15 (1): 141–177.

Masumoto, N. (1994) 'Interpretations of the Filmed Body: An Analysis of the Japanese Version of Leni Riefenstahl's Olympia', in R.K. Barney, and K.V. Meier (eds), *Critical Reflections on Olympic Ideology*. London, Ontario: University of Western Ontario, pp. 146–58.

May, V. (1995) 'Environmental Implications of the 1992 Winter Olympic Games', *Tourism Management*, 16(4): 269–275.

Miah, A. (2004) *Genetically Modified Athletes: Biomedical Ethics, Gene Doping and Sport*. Abingdon: Routledge.

——(2011) 'media2012: Media Blueprint for London 2012', *Culture & the Olympics* 13(1): 1–6. Available online: http://www.culturalolympics.org.uk/wp-content/uploads/2011/07/Miah2011MediaBlueprintC@tO.pdf (accessed 21 May 2011).

Miah, A., García, B. and Zhihui, T. (2008) '"We are the Media": Non-Accredited Media and Citizen Journalists at the Olympic Games', in M.E. Price and D. Dayan (eds) *Owning the Olympics: Narratives of the New China*. Ann Arbor: University of Michigan Press, pp. 320–45.

Miah, A. and Jones, J. (2012) 'The Olympic Movement's New Media Revolution: Monetization, Open Media and Intellectual Property', in S. Wagg and H. Lenskyj (eds) *A Handbook of Olympic Studies*. Basingstoke: Palgrave-Macmillan.

Michaelis, V. (2009) 'USOC, IOC reach interim compromise on revenue deal', *USA Today*, 27 March. Available online: http://www.usatoday.com/sports/olympics/2009-03-27-ioc-temporary-deal_N.htm (accessed 3 September 2011).

Miller, D. (1992) *Olympic Revolution: The Olympic Biography of Juan Antonio Samaranch*. London: Pavilion.

Miller, S. (2006) *Ancient Greek Athletics*. New Haven, CT: Yale University Press

Min, G. (1987) 'Over-Commercialization of the Olympics 1988: The Role of U.S. Television Networks', *International Review for the Sociology of Sport* 22(2): 137–42.

Moon, B.-K. (2009, October 5) 'Secretary-General's Address to Olympic Congress in Copenhagen (SG/SM/12514)', *United Nations*. Available online: http://www.un.org/News/Press/docs/2009/sgsm12514.doc.htm (accessed 21 May 2011).

Moragas, M. (1988) 'Local Culture and International Audience Facing Barcelona'92', in S.P. Kang, J. MacAloon, and R. DaMatta (eds) *The Olympics and East/West and South/North Cultural Exchange*. Seoul: The Institute for Ethnological Studies, Hanyang University, pp. 753–71.

——(1992) *Los Juegos de la Comunicación. Las múltiples dimensiones comunicativas de los Juegos Olímpicos*. Madrid: Fundesco.

Moragas, M., MacAloon, J. Llinés, M. (eds) (1995) *Olympic Ceremonies: Historical Continuity and Cultural Exchange*. Proceedings of International Symposium on Olympic Ceremonies. Lausanne: International Olympic Committee.

Moragas, M., Rivenburgh, N.K., and Larson, F. (1995) *Television in the Olympics*. John Libbey: London.

Moragas, M., Kennett, C. and Puig, N. (eds) (2002) *The Legacy of the Olympic Games, 1984–2000*. Lausanne: IOC.

Moreno, A.B., Moragas, M. and Paniagua, R. (1999) 'The Evolution of Volunteers at the Olympic Games', *Papers of the Symposium Volunteers, Global*

Society and the Olympic Movement. Autonomous University of Barcelona. Available online: http://olympicstudies.uab.es/volunteers/moreno.html (accessed 21 May 2011).

Morris, A. (1999). '"I Can Compete!" China in the Olympic Games, 1932 and 1936', *Journal of Sport History*, 26(3): 545–66.

Morton, J. (dir) (2011) *Twenty Twelve*. British Broadcasting Corporation.

Murphy, B. (2004) 'Greeks give the Games an Epic Welcome Home', *The Scotsman*. Available online: http://sport.scotsman.com/top-stories/Greeks-give-the-Games-an.2554598.jp# (accessed 9 July 2011).

Muller, N. (2004) 'Olympic Education', *The Sport Journal* 7 (1). Available online: http://www.thesportjournal.org/article/olympic-education.

Multicultural Arts Alliance (1999) *The Future of Multicultural Arts*. Sydney: Australian Museum (7 November).

Nauright, J. and Magdalinski, T. (2000) 'Selling the "Spirit of the Dream": Olympologies and the Corporate Invasion of the Classroom', in J. Tolleneer and R. Renson (eds) *Old Borders, New Borders, No Borders: Sport and Physical Education in a Period of Change*. Aachen: Meyer and Meyer, pp. 431–40.

Niccol, A. (1997) *GATTACA*. Columbia Pictures.

Olympic Solidarity (2006) *Olympic Solidarity: Creation and Development*. Lausanne: IOC.

Olympic Solidarity (2009) *Quadrennial Plan*. Lausanne: IOC. Available Online: <http://www.olympic.org/Documents/PDF_files_0807/os_2009_2012_en.pdf> (accessed 3 September 2011).

Paul, D., 2004. 'World Cities as Hegemonic Projects: The Politics of Global Imagineering in Montreal', *Political Geography* 23(5): 571–96.

Payne, M. (2006) *Olympic Turnaround*. Westport, CT: Praeger.

Penn Museum (2011) *The Real Story of the Ancient Olympic Games*. Available online: http://www.penn.museum/sites/olympics/olympicathletes.shtml# (last accessed February 2011)

Permezel, B. (2000) *The Games, Series 2*. Australian Broadcasting Corporation.

Pitsula, J.M. (2004) 'The Nazi Olympics: A Reinterpretation', *Olympika: The International Journal of Olympic Studies* 13: 1–26.

Pound, R.W. (1994) *Five Rings over Korea: The Secret Negotiations Behind the 1988 Olympic Games in Seoul*. Boston: Little, Brown and Co.

Pound, R. (2003) *Olympic Games Study Commission*. Lausanne: IOC. Available online: http://www.olympic.org/Documents/Reports/EN/en_report_725.pdf (accessed 21 May 2011).

Preuss, H. (2002) 'Rarely Considered Economic Legacies of Olympic Games', in M. Moragas, C. Kennett and N. Puig (eds) *The Legacy of the Olympic Games 1984–2000*. Lausanne: IOC, pp. 243–52.

——(2006) *The Economics of Staging the Olympics: A Comparison of the Games 1972–2008*. Cheltenham: Edward Elgar Publishing Limited.

———(2007) *The Impact and Evaluation of Major Sporting Events*. London: Routledge.

Preuss, H. and Solberg, H.A. (2006) 'Attracting Major Sporting Events: The Role of Local Residents', *European Sport Management Quarterly*, 6(4): 391–411.

Price, M.E. and Dayan, D. (eds) (2008) *Owning the Olympics: Narratives of the New China*. Ann Arbor: University of Michigan Press.

Quoqi, X. (2008) *Olympic Dreams: China and Sports 1895–2008*. Cambridge, MA: Harvard University Press.

Randall, C. and Helm, T. (2006) 'Blair Won the Olympics by Flouting Rules, Claim French', *The Telegraph*. Available online: http://www.telegraph.co.uk/news/uknews/1516271/Blair-won-the-Olympics-by-flouting-rules-claim-French.html (accessed 1 July 2011).

Reeve, S. (2000) *One Day in September*. New York: Arcade Publishing.

Richards, A., Fussey, P. and Silke, A. (eds) (2011). *Terrorism and the Olympics*. Abingdon and New York: Routledge.

Roche, Maurice. (2000) *Mega-events and Modernity: Olympics and Expos in the Growth of Global Culture*. London: Routledge.

———(2002) 'The Olympics and "Global Citizenship"', *Citizenship Studies*, 6(2): 165–81.

Rodriguez, K. (2011) 'Privacy in the Wake of Olympic Security: Wikileaks sheds Light on How the U.S. Pressured Brazil', *Electronic Frontier Foundation*. Available online: http://www.eff.org/deeplinks/2011/02/wikileaks-Olympic-Security-Wikileaks-Sheds-Light-How-US-Pressured-Brazil+ (accessed 26 June 2011).

Rogge, J. (2002a) *Speech by the IOC President at the Opening Ceremony of the 114th IOC Session In Mexico City*, IOC, Report no. 593, Bellas Artes, Mexico. Available online: http://www.olympic.org/Documents/Reports/EN/en_report_593.pdf

———(2002b) 'Message from the President of the International Olympic Committee', in M. Moragas, C. Kennett and N. Puig (eds) *The Legacy of the Olympic Games 1984–2000*. Lausanne: IOC, p. 13.

———(2008a) 'Full Text of Speech by IOC President at Beijing Olympics Closing', *Embassy of the Peoples Republic of China in the United States*. Available online: http://www.china-embassy.org/eng/zt/768675/t486638.htm (accessed 21 May 2011).

———(2008b) *Advancing the Games: The IOC, London 2012 and the Future of de Coubertin's Olympic Movement.*, Pierre de Coubertin lecture, RSA London. Available online: http://www.london2012.com/documents/culture/jacques-rogge-2008-de-coubertin-speech.pdf (accessed 3 September 2011).

Romney, M. (2004) *Turnaround: Crisis, Leadership and the Olympic Games*. Washington, D.C.: Regenery Publishing.

Roult, R. and Lefebvre, S. (2010) 'Planning and Reconversion of Olympic Heritages: The Montreal Olympic Stadium', *The International Journal of the History of Sport*, 27(16-18): 2731–47.

Rudolph, E. (2005) 'Full Text of Eric Rudolph's Confession'. *National Public Radio*. Available online: http://www.npr.org/templates/story/story.php?storyId=4600480# (accessed 2 July 2011).

Sanko, J. (1999) 'Colorado Only State Ever to Turn Down Olympics', *Rocky Mountain News*, October 12 Available online: http://www.gamesmonitor.org.uk/node/546 (accessed 21 May 2011).

Scherer, J. and Whitson, D. (2009) 'Public Broadcasting, Sport and Cultural Citizenship: The Future of Sport on the Canadian Broadcasting Corporation?', *International Review for Sociology of Sport*, 44 (2-3): 213-29.

Schiller, K. and Young, C. (2010) 'Motion and Landscape: Otl Aicher, Günther Grzimek and the Graphic and Garden Designs of the 1972 Munich Olympics', *Urban History*, 37: 272–88.

Schneider, R.C. and Stier. W.F. (2001) 'Leni Riefenstahl's "Olympia": Brilliant Cinematography or Nazi Propaganda?', *The Sport Journal* 4. Available online: <http://www.thesportjournal.org/article/leni-riefenstahls-olympia-brilliant-cinematography-or-nazi-propaganda (accessed 4 September 2011).

Segrave, J. O. (2000) 'The Modern Olympic Games: An Access to Ontology', *Quest*, 48(1): 57–66.

Sharp, R. (2011) 'Nationwide British arts festival set for Brazil'. *The Independent*. Available online: http://blogs.independent.co.uk/2011/06/12/nationwide-british-arts-festival-set-for-brazil/ (accessed 24 July 2011).

Simson, V. and Jennings, A. (1992) *The Lords of the Rings*. New York: Simon & Schuster.

Sinclair, I. (2011) *Ghost Milk: Calling Time on the Grand Project*. London: Hamish Hamilton.

Spilling (1998) 'Beyond Intermezzo? On the Long-Term Industrial Impacts of Mega-Events: The Case of Lillehammer 1994', *Festival Management and Event Tourism*, 5(3): 101–22.

Spielberg, S. (2006) *Munich*. Amblin Entertainment.

Stanton, R. (2000) *The Forgotten Olympic Art Competitions: The Story of the Olympic Art Competitions of the 20th Century*. Victoria: Trafford.

Sullivan, S.O. and Mechikoff, R.A. (2004) 'A Man of his Time: Pierre de Coubertin's Olympic Ideology and the Via Media', *Olympika: The International Journal of Olympic Studies* 13:27–52.

Surveillance Studies Centre (2009) 'The Vancouver Statement of Surveillance, Security and Privacy Researchers about the Vancouver 2010 Olympic Winter Games', *The New Transparency*, Surveillance Studies Centre, Canada. Available online: http://www.sscqueens.org/Vancouver_Statement (accessed 2 September 2011).

Sydney Bid Ltd (1992) 'Cultural Program and Youth Camp', in *Sydney Bid Books*. Sydney: Sydney Bid Ltd.

Titmuss, R. (1977) *The Gift Relationship: From Human Blood to Social Policy.* John Ashton and Ann Oakley. London: LSE Books.

Tomlinson, A. (1996) 'Olympic Spectacle: Opening Ceremonies and Some Paradoxes of Globalization', *Media, Culture & Society* 18(4): 583–602.

Toohey, K. and Taylor, T. (2008) 'Mega Events, Fear, and Risk: Terrorism at the Olympic Games', *Journal of Sport Management* 22: 451–469.

Toohey, K. and Veal, A.J. (2007) *The Olympic Games: A Social Science Perspective, 2nd Edition.*, Wallingford: CABI.

Toohey, K. and Warning, P. (1998) 'Olympic Flames: Analysis of an Olympic Internet Newsgroup', in R.K. Barney, K.B. Wamsley, S.G. Martyn, and G.H. MacDonald (eds) *Global and Cultural Critique: Problematizing the Olympic Games.* University of Western Ontario: Centre for Olympic Studies.

Torres, C. (2010) 'The Youth Olympic Games, Their Programs, and Olympism'. *Paper to the International Olympic Committee Postgraduate Grant Selection Committee.* Available online: http://doc.rero.ch/lm.php?url=1000,42,38,20110314150357-KM/2010_-_Torres.pdf (accessed April 2011).

United Nations Environmental Programme (2009) *Independent Environmental Assessment: Beijing 2008 Olympic Games*, Geneva, United Nations. Available online: http://unep.org/pdf/BEIJING_REPORT_COMPLETE.pdf (accessed 21 May 2011).

United Nations (2011) 'Brazil Off-course for World Cup and Olympics – UN housing expert'. *Office of the High Commissioner for Human Rights.* Available online: http://www.ohchr.org/EN/NewsEvents/Pages/DisplayNews.aspx?NewsID=10960&LangID=E# (accessed 3 July 2011).

United States Government Accountability Office (2005) *Olympic Security: U.S. Support to Athens Games Provides Lessons for Future Olympics. Report to Congressional Requesters (GAO-05-547)*, Washington D.C. Available online: http://www.gao.gov/new.items/d05547.pdf (accessed 21 May 2011).

United States Presidents Council on Bioethics (2003) *Beyond Therapy: Biotechnology and the Pursuit of Happiness.*

University of East London and the Thames Gateway Institute for Sustainability (2010) *Olympic Games Impact Study: London 2012 Pre-Games Report*, Available online: http://www.uel.ac.uk/geo-information/documents/UEL_TGIfS_Pre Games_OGI_Release.pdf (accessed 21 May 2011).

VanWynsberghe, R. and Ritchie, I. (1994) '(Ir)relevant Rings: The Symbolic Consumption of the Olympic Logo in Postmodern Media Culture', in R.K. Barney and R.K. Meier (eds) *Critical Reflections on Olympic Ideology.* London, Ontario: University of Western Ontario, pp. 124–35.

Verdaguer, C. (1995) 'Mega-events: Local Strategies and Global Tourist Attractions', in A. Montanari and A. Williams (eds) *European Tourism.* Chichester and New York: Wiley.

Vidal, J. and Gibson, O. (2011) 'London Olympics Pollution on Course to Land Britain Hefty Fine from IOC', *The Guardian*, 24 April. Available online: *http:// www.guardian.co.uk/environment/2011/apr/24/london-olympics-pollution-fine-ioc* (accessed 21 May 2011).

Weed, M. (2008) *Olympic Tourism*. Oxford: Butterworth-Heinemann.

Wenn, S.R. (1993) 'Lights! Camera! Little Action: Television, Avery Brundage and the 1956 Melbourne Olympics', *Sporting Traditions* 10(1): 38–39.

The White House (1984) 'Los Angeles Olympic Games Counterintelligence and Security Precautions,' *National Security Decision, Directive Number 135,* Washington, D.C. Available online: http://www.fas.org/irp/offdocs/nsdd/nsdd-135.pdf (accessed 21 May 2011).

Whitson, D. (1998) 'Olympic Sport, Global Media and Cultural Diversity', in R. Barney, K.B. Wamsley, S.G. Martyn, and G.H. MacDonald (eds) *Global and Cultural Critique: Problematizing the Olympic Games*. University of Western Ontario: Centre for Olympic Studies, pp. 1–9.

Whyte, D. (2000) 'Athens 2004 in Serious Danger, Says Samaranch', *The Independent*. Available online: http://www.independent.co.uk/sport/general/athens-2004-in-serious-danger-says-samaranch-720432.html (accessed 31 August, 2011).

World Intellectual Property Organization (1981) *The Nairobi Treaty on the Protection of the Olympic Symbol*. Available online: http://www.wipo.int/treaties/en/ip/nairobi/pdf/trtdocs_wo018.pdf (accessed 21 May 2011).

World Wildlife Fund (2004) *Environmental Assessment of the Athens 2004 Olympic Games*, Available online: http://assets.panda.org/downloads/olympicsscor ecardenglish.doc (accessed 21 May 2011).

Xin, X. (2006) 'Modernizing China in the Olympic Spotlight: China's National Identity and the 2008 Beijing Olympiad', *The Sociological Review*, 54(2): 90–107.

Young, David C. (1985) 'Coubertin and the Olympic Logo', in J.A. Mangan (ed.) *Proceedings of the XIth HISPA International Congress*, Glasgow: Jordan Hill College, pp. 326–27.

Zelizer, B. and Allen, S. (eds) (2002) *Journalism after September 11*. London: Routledge.

INDEX